The

Beggar

Dedication

To

Dodie Cheairs

The Beggar

Ralph Lewis

ISBN # 978-0-692-06577-8

Preface

Before reading a book it is reasonable to ask, "What is the book about?" This book is about the world of a professional fundraiser. It is about the actions and issues that can confront anyone responsible for soliciting money to fund the operation of a charity. It is about my world.

Over the past twelve years I have written hundreds of appeals, newsletter articles and thank you letters. In those cases I was not writing for myself but for the agency where I work, explaining it, praising it, and encouraging others to support it. While this writing was not always easy, it was a process that I adjusted to. Besides, very little of my writing for the agency, went out without editing by other people. If I wrote badly it was corrected and if I felt strongly about a statement, I had to overcome other's resistance to it. In the final analysis, the agency was a place I completely believed in and I was happy and proud to speak for. That sort of confidence helps anyone's communication skills.

In this book I am trying something different. I do not wish to write another "how to" book for the fundraising profession or even a book to help volunteers and neophytes. There are plenty of fine books available by people much more knowledgeable and successful in fundraising than me. Instead, I want to act as a kind of every-man voice for anyone who solicits money for his or her favorite charity. Whether this person is a volunteer or professional, they represent a field of endeavor in America essential to its well being and at the core of its glory. I also want to give insight to the general public about a world that our society depends on and trusts but may not understand very well. The various chapters have been written at different times and on a range of topics by which I have tried to give some understanding to issues in the nonprofit world. At the same time I am only one person reflecting my experiences and understanding of the events and issues around me.

Over the last several years, charities have had a difficult time. Less and less is publicly said about what they accomplish and much is said about what they do wrong. Government at every level reduces programs and sends more of the needy to private charities for help; while it also tries to gain revenue from the same charities and forces more burdensome regulations on their already stretched resources. This situation would not exist if government did not have the acceptance, if not the support, of the American people to this new attitude towards charities. As to whether this trend is a direct reaction to what charity is all about, public ignorance of the situation or merely that charities are the latest institution to feel the poison of America's desolation and cynicism toward all its institutions is impossible to say. What can be said is that all is not well.

However, charity is still strong, and people who could easily make more money in the business world often stay in nonprofit work. These people believe in what they are doing, but they are just as human as everyone else. They get tired, frustrated, and sometimes burned out, just like everyone else. In some ways it can be worse in charity work. Since the cause is so important one can feel much worse about not always giving 100%. Yet charities still do a great job and are routinely shown, in national surveys, to be more cost effective and more respected than either the public or for-profit sector.

The general public needs to see the commonality of experience they have with fundraisers. By speaking for my profession I hope to demonstrate this commonality. If most of my fellow professionals read what I have written and conclude that I am a moronic windbag, I must respond, Amen. If, however, a few of my fellow professionals receive some degree of appreciation from donors as a result of my thoughts then I have not failed. Finally, my purpose is to give my fellow workers a sense that they are not alone. Comradeship is a great deterrent to exhaustion and despair. All charity is done in community, for you cannot give love in isolation. The more the public can understand these people, this profession and the world of charity in general, the more likely they are to support and protect this vital resource.

As I have worked on this book I have come to realize it is both an explanation of a profession and a personal spiritual journey. Much of my understanding of the emotional and ethical issues confronted by fundraisers is colored by my own religious beliefs. I make no apology for this and hope it will aid in understanding the motivation of many who work in fundraising. No religion has a monopoly on charity or on ethics. I try to offer as broad a view as possible so that this work can speak to the widest range of people. I also try to separate out those issues and viewpoints that may only relate to those who share my faith (Christianity) from some of the broader positions in modern America. If you have never been inside a church and never plan to go there, this book will still help you understand the world of charity. I am not writing to Christians but to donors. For that matter I am writing to anyone just curious about charities. My faith and my work tend to intertwine. I think this is true for everyone no matter how they view the world. Faith colors our actions and reactions to all parts of life. If you will bear with me I feel you will find we have some things in common.

I am writing this in isolation. As I write this there are only a few people who know I am writing a book. It must be this way for me to continue because I know it does not matter what I think of this writing. For this to be anything more than my own ego a publisher has to decide to take a chance on what I have written and publish it. But that is no different than when any development staffer sends out an appeal letter. Until the donations come in, we don't know if we wrote well or badly. And in my case, I sometimes wonder, did they give because of what I wrote or in spite of it. Donors are very generous.

Chapter 1 Begging 101

"It is an ancient Mariner, and he stoppeth one of three."

Rime of the Ancient Mariner

Samuel Taylor Coleridge (English Poet)

He approached me on the street. "Hey man, can you help me out? I need money for a bus pass so I can get to work." We were only half a block from a well-known homeless shelter. He must have realized the ridiculous nature of a request for help with help so close by. "They won't help me unless I join their church. I don't want to join no church; I just want to get to work."

I handed over the loose change in my pocket (my general response to street beggars) and he began to explain it was not enough. "I need three dollars," he said. I brushed him off with the standard reply "That's all I have." I felt fairly sure we were lying to each other. I did have more money in my wallet but the three quarters I had handed over was the limit of my willingness to get involved. I moved away with a meaningless "Take care of yourself," and he gave me an "OK man," as he moved toward someone else coming up the street.

I have seen him in the same general location two or three times since and, strangely enough this has made me feel pretty good. For one thing it has relived my conscience about the remote possibility that he really was in crisis and might lose his job. If he was working the same spot, then whatever his problems were three dollars, from me, would not solve them. I can hide behind the attitude of helplessness toward a problem too big to solve with a quick fix. I believe this is the reaction of most people toward poverty and suffering.

I try to avoid having the painful resentment that afflicts so many people. The resentment coined in the phrase "I am not about to waste my hard earned money on some lazy bum who will only use it for booze or drugs". I recognize that money given to a street beggar may very well go for liquor or drugs. First, I figure alcoholism or drug addiction is a real thing, and not to be dismissed with high minded words about cleaning one's self-up. I would much rather he was shaking me down for loose change than hitting someone in the head and stealing their purse. Second, while I reject the concept that all ills are society's fault and there is no such thing as individual responsibility, I understand that poverty is not a minor disruption on the path to wealth and fame, but a gigantic obstacle that can be overcome only by great strength of character, or by very good fortune. People who rise above poverty are often noticed because it is not that common. You do not have to be lazy to be poor. Misfortune will do a fine job of putting you there and keeping you there, and begging will not make you rich. I know there are many stories of beggars who make thousands and thousands of dollars. I know because people who never give to help the poor have often bent my ear with these stories as justification for their parsimony.

The reality is that poor is poor. It is not much fun and often a beggar in his own way is showing something of a creative and enterprising spirit by hustling himself in a very hard sell market.

This brings us to the third reason I felt good about my encounter with that particular beggar. I liked his sales pitch. The bus pass story told me he had a job and was trying to keep it. He was telling me his was a temporary problem that my three dollars would correct. It was a good pitch.

I like a good pitch. I happen to be a professional beggar myself and have been one for over fifteen years. Welcome to my world.

Chapter 2 Development

"Shut not thy purse strings always against painted distress."

Complaint of the Decay of Beggars in the Metropolis

Charles Lamb (English essayist)

Yes, I am a beggar. The job has an official title, Director of Development, but I am a beggar none the less. I work for a charity in a major city. As with most charities, much of what we offer to our clients is free. We cannot sell the services we provide because they are services to help the poor and by definition the poor have little or no money. It follows that they cannot pay for the services we offer them. In order to keep the doors open, to pay the staff's wages, the utility bills and the rest of the expenses we must have money given to us. My job is to get people, businesses, foundations, churches and other groups to donate money, goods and volunteer time. No donations mean no free services, so we beg for help.

Some people in Development do not like the term "begging". They feel that it is a pejorative term that conjures up the image of a whining vagabond like my panhandling friend in the last chapter. I have heard several talks in which an experienced fundraiser has said, "I explain the needs of my agency and point out the opportunity the prospective donor has of doing good and then let him or her decide to help. I do not beg as that would be demeaning and false."

This philosophy has a couple of problems. First, the salesman in me spots the common problem of being unable to close the deal. Sales managers all over will tell you that training a sales person to "ask for the order" is a major difficulty in selling. People do not ask because they fear rejection. Most people have a major problem with the word "no". They take it as a personal rejection of themselves or they think of it as an absolute that closes and locks a door forever. "If he says 'no', than there is nothing more I can say or do." This is an odd view when you consider how unimpressed we were with "no" as children.

For example, here is a sample conversation. "Mommy can I have a cookie?"

"No."

"Please Mommy can't I have a cookie?"

"No! I said no."

"Mommy, I really want a cookie. Please!"

"I said no and I meant no. Maybe you can have one after dinner."

"Oh Mommy, just one cookie!"

"No! Now go away, you are about to get in trouble with me."

"PLEASE MOMMY!"

"No young man! Now go away!"

"But mommy..." etc. etc. etc.

We have all had or heard that conversation sometime in the past. The child may or may not get the cookie and he may get a swat in the pants, still he keeps on pitching. He never lets "no" end the negotiation. Yet when we become adults we want to grant "no" a solemn sacred position in our language. Good sales people understand that "no" only means "no for now" or "no" to what you just said. You can always say something different or say it at another time. The important thing is to keep asking.

Charity work is much the same. You have to ask for the gift. You may need to ask for some information first. Are you asking for a gift that they have the ability to give? Would another size or type of gift be more appropriate? And so on and so forth as needed. Regardless of your approach, the person is entitled to the courtesy of a formal request. This is a gift they are giving, not a tax they must pay.

The second problem with the idea that there is something wrong with begging is based on my understanding of some aspects of Christianity. I understand there are many people who do much charitable work without being Christian or even Theistic. Love is a universal truth and can be found in all major religions. However, I focus on Christianity because first, I am one, and second, I am more familiar with Christian texts than with the other religions. While I own translations of the Koran, some of the teachings of Buddha, various Hindu texts, the Tao Te Ching and the Book of Mormon, my Bible is much more dog-eared. I can work best in the context of what I know and believe. As a result, I address moral and ethical issues about begging in a Christian context. I believe the problem begging is for some people in Development an issue of pride. Fundraisers, just like most people, do not like to humble themselves by asking for help. However, pride is not a virtue but a vice in the eyes of most major religions. To set one's own pride as more important than the charity one is supposedly helping is very human but may also be disloyal to the charity. To work effectively in this line of work one may have to sacrifice a bit of personal pride. I know I have plenty to spare.

Anyway, it is time to plunge ahead into the dark world of Beggarland with gun and camera. Off we go.

Chapter 3 The Basics of Begging

"Wise are those who learn that the bottom line doesn't always have to be their top priority."
William A. Ward (inspirational writer)

Fundraising has some basic aspects that the general public, many donors and even some fundraising professionals do not seem to understand. There is nothing unusual in this misunderstanding. Most lines of work have aspects to them that only their professionals understand. Those on the outside are puzzled, angered or amused by these things depending on their perception, misperception and personalities.

I remember hearing a retired army officer responding to the question of why you have to march, salute, and shine your shoes in the military. The questioner also wanted to know why everyone in a training unit got punished when one person made a mistake. The officer said that the army understood much of what a recruit did in basic training was unreasonable and petty. He said that 90% of all men so trained, would gain the army nothing. Yet the other 10% of the recruits might some day find themselves in battle and the training would pay off. The whole purpose of having men do stupid things automatically when ordered was to get them to do very dangerous things automatically when ordered in battle. On a battlefield there is no time for explanation and argument. All those other seemingly needless things pay off, if you do what you are told when you are under fire. He also said group punishment and reward was to get recruits used to working for the best interests of their teammates. They come to count on each other. Once again, in the unlikely event they are in combat, the army does not believe the average soldier will continue to risk their life for the flag, mother, and country. However, soldiers will risk death for the welfare of their teammates if they have come to value and depend on them on a regular basis. The person asking the question said the officer's statement made it possible to understand something that had not made much sense before.

In a matter as simple as an interview, a reporter, a psychiatrist, and a salesman will each have a completely different approach and purpose. That does not mean any of them are doing it wrong. You have to understand their jobs to comprehend the reasons for the differences. Hopefully this will help people understand why charities do things in such a seemingly odd way. For example, why do we keep mailing out items, such as newsletters, appeals and gift acknowledgements when they cost money and we are always complaining about a lack of money? The reason is that people will stop giving if we stop asking. One of the major factors in why people stop giving is because they feel the charity is no longer interested in them. There are all sorts of good causes out there asking for help and if a person feels the charity has lost interest in them then that person will help elsewhere. All of the newsletters and reports are to keep people informed as to where their money is going.

One major misconception is that charities want to send mail to individuals even if they don't want it. Currently, there is a lot of legislation being passed to protect people from unwanted solicitations by phone, email and regular mail. Sadly, a few charities have made national news for being involved in heavy-handed solicitation tactics. Yet, the vast majority of charities do not want to contact people who do not want to support them. To do so costs the charities money and man-hours to send information to people who are annoyed by receiving it. Unlike some giant for-profit mailing houses, which may have no mechanism in place to remove names from a mailing list, charities generally can and will remove these names. It may take time to get a name off a list, and in the interim the person may get another mailing, but generally the name will be removed. A little patience and forbearance will go a long way.

It also helps to use good sense. I had one person send back one of our standard return envelops from a mass mailing, with a note asking us to remove his mother's name from our mailing list because she was dead. Unfortunately, he did not sign the note or mention his mother's name. There was no way my staff could find out who it was from because we had sent out several thousand appeals with this standard return envelope. Sure enough, about three months later we sent out another appeal and got back another envelope asking us to remove "mother" from the mailing list. Again, there was no name or return address to guide us. Finally, about six months later a third appeal produced a third, and this time angry note, telling us we were ignoring repeated requests to remove "my mother" from the mailing list. As before, there was no name or address. I am in complete sympathy with this person, for he or she had every reason to think my staff members are insensitive clods. Many people go through life calling their parents Mother and Father and never addressing them by their name. The loss of one's parent can be a horrible blow and no one wants to be reminded of it by some stupid charity and yet, this person has no idea how much we wanted to stop mailing to "Mother". The situation finally ended because we stop mailing to people who do not respond, and the mother's name undoubtedly came up as "no response". To this day, I feel confident her child is out there, telling everyone how stupid and insensitive my agency is.

Then there are people who only want mail, and cannot understand why we bother with all the work and cost of fundraising events. Those auctions, fashion shows, dinners, golf tournaments, car washes, bike-athons and all the rest exhaust staff and volunteers alike. The simple answer is that people like them. They are often a better device for introducing new people to the charity than a letter. It is, after all, a kind of party and most people like parties. Unfortunately there are a lot more people who like to go to parties than like to organize them, but as long as people will come to fundraisers and pay money, charities will have such activities.

The basic reason for a charity to do anything is to raise money. Non profit business does not mean broke business. It is in the absence of profit to owners and stockholders that it differs from other businesses. If it goes out of business it stops helping people. It helps to keep this fact in mind when trying to understand fund raising.

Finally, if a donor's favorite charity is doing something they do not understand it is fine to ask why. Donors are not guaranteed charities will change something the donor doesn't like, but the donor is entitled to a response to stated concerns. If one cares enough to give, it is reasonable that one cares enough to inquire. Any good charity wants feedback from the donors. If you think you can help your favorite charity by your inquiries and recommendations, then by all means, take action. But beware: that is sometimes how people wind up elected to the board of directors and taking on all the work and responsibility that goes with the title.

Chapter 4 The Story of Giving

"No man is an island, entire of itself...any man's death diminishes me, because I am involved in mankind;"
Meditation XVII
John Donne (English metaphysical poet and churchman)

In the tenth chapter of the Gospel of Luke a lawyer asked Jesus, "What must I do to inherit eternal life?" Jesus then asked the lawyer what he thought the law said about the issue. The lawyer replied "Love the Lord your God with all your heart, with all your soul, with all your strength, and with all your mind; and your neighbor as yourself." (Oxford English translation)

Jesus told the man he was right and if he would do that he would gain eternal life. The lawyer then asked, "Who is my neighbor?" Jesus replied "A man was on his way from Jerusalem down to Jericho..." And began the telling of what has become the most famous story of charity in the world, that of the Good Samaritan.

The image of charity that Jesus drew on in this story was nothing new to the Jews. Their religion was unusual in its proactive stand concerning the duty of charity towards others, especially widows and strangers, who could not repay kindness. The Torah dictates very clear requirements to the Jews to provide generously for others in need. Examples of this can be found in Leviticus 19:10, "And thou shalt not glean thy vineyard, neither shalt thou gather every grape of thy vineyard; thou shalt leave them for the poor and stranger: I am the LORD your God." (King James Bible) 19:33 "And if a stranger sojourn with thee in your land, ye shall not do him wrong." (American Standard Version) or 23:22 "When you reap the harvest of your land, you shall not wholly reap into the corners of your field, neither shall you gather the gleanings of your harvest: you shall leave them for the poor, and for the foreigner. I am Yahweh your God." (World English

Bible) as well as Deuteronomy 15:7 "If in any of your towns in the land which the Lord your God is giving you, there is a poor man, one of your countrymen, do not let your heart be hard or your hand shut to him;" (Bible in Basic English) and 24:14-15 "Thou shalt not refuse the hire of the needy, and the poor, whether he be thy brother, or a stranger that dwelleth with thee in the land, and is within thy gates: But thou shalt pay him the price of his labour the same day, before the going down of the sun, because he is poor, and with it maintaineth his life: lest he cry against thee to the Lord, and it be reputed to thee for a sin" (Douay-Rheims Bible)   This attitude of charity was not all that common in ancient times; for while most of the religions of the ancient world often had punishments from the gods for those who persecuted the weak or oppressed visitors, there was little about special offerings for other human's welfare. The gods generally only demanded such offerings for themselves. In some cases, where human sacrifices were called for, they were only too happy to have strangers, prisoners, women and children killed. For the Jews, God told them he expected them to care for the down and out because they themselves had been slaves in Egypt and should have sympathy with suffering.

Sympathy is a basic catalyst to charity. We cannot feel cold and indifferent to other's suffering if we are going to act to help them. In many cases, the challenge to being sympathetic is that we are wrapped up in our own lives and do not want to see this suffering. The people, who passed by the beaten man before the Samaritan came to help are examples of people not wanting to see. True sympathy toward other's suffering is painful. If you get involved enough with others to sympathize, it means you must feel some of their pain. Pain is terrible and we in America avoid it at all costs, even at the cost of loosing some of our own humanity. Pain is not an avoidable option, but a universal reality.

I still remember my first real introduction to what life was really like for the clients at the agency. I had been hired as the agency's first development director only two months previous. I had made the transition from the for-profit to the non-profit sector a couple of years earlier and had enjoyed the work I had done with several institutions. At the same time this was my first opportunity to set up a new department in a social service agency and I felt both excited and overwhelmed. The staff had been very friendly but I was still finding my way, and often I felt unsure what to do with myself.

It was the middle of December and we were running our Christmas shop. Each year the agency set up a free store for neighborhood residents. A parent (generally the mother) registered the family with us and then was able to come on an assigned day, at an assigned time, to shop for a prescribed number of gifts for each member of the family. The gifts are always new and there is a wide selection of toys, clothes and small household items to pick from. We found a long time ago that it is better to let a mother shop for her family rather than to pick items ourselves because Mom knows best. This is a very labor-intensive week for us, involving hundreds of volunteers and families.

I was sitting at my desk when the receptionist asked if I could help a client. Normally, I do not get involved with the clients other than to say hello and chat. The program staff is trained to help the clients and I am not. But I was new on the job and had some free time as often happens to a new person in a busy place. I agreed to see if I could help. There was a woman sitting in the lobby surrounded by half a dozen grocery bags and it was clear she had just finished her turn shopping in our Christmas shop. The receptionist explained the woman needed a ride back to her apartment in the public housing project a couple of blocks away. I could see there was something wrong because the lady had her head bent down but I could see her face looked exhausted and was perspiring heavily. When she rose it was clear from her expression and halting movement that she was in pain. We generally are too short staffed at the Christmas shop to provide rides so we normally do not offer them but this woman clearly needed help so I agreed to drive her over to her apartment. Our clients are low-income individuals and families from the inner city. Transportation is always an issue to such people because a car is not normally affordable. Families at the Christmas shop must make some arrangements of their own to get back home with their gifts and over the years this has worked itself out. However, this woman had walked over from her home and now was not able to walk back with her packages.

I was not very happy with this assignment at the time. The woman was clearly sick and I was concerned about catching whatever she had. Also, the public housing project where she lived had a very bad reputation and I did not want to go there. Nonetheless, I helped her into my car and off we went.

The housing project was worse than I had realized. It was about noon and there was an alcoholic sleeping on the ground in front of the entrance. The hallway was dark and dirty and the elevator smelled strongly of urine. I got the woman into her apartment and left as fast as I could. We had hardly spoken the entire time.

Back at the office I asked the receptionist what the story was on this woman, wanting to know if I could expect to come down with the flu in a few days. The story was not what I expected. The woman had just checked herself out of the hospital where she had undergone kidney surgery two days before. She had left against her doctor's advice because she had to return home and care for her children. There was no one she could rely one to make sure they were all right. This was the day she had been assigned a time to shop. She had walked over from her apartment two days after her surgery, walked through the Christmas shop and picked out her children's gifts, and collapsed in our lobby from pain and exhaustion. Walking back home had been more than she could do.

I went back to my desk ashamed. I had thought I was doing a big thing carrying this woman's packages without complaint while she had carried herself in uncomplaining agony. I had spent a few minutes in a dirty and dangerous place while she had to live there. I was a mere witness to an act of courage and parental devotion greater than I had ever seen.

I got the message then and there. I had the responsibility of raising money to enable the staff to help people like her and I have never forgotten it. The responsibility of this job can sometimes feel overwhelming. No one ever criticizes me or blames me but in years when the finances are low and the staff has to do without I feel the weight of my job.

I have told this story to many groups over the years and I still have a strong sense of emotion when I do. It is a real honor to work in a field where you can help and a real burden when you see how much help is needed. Beggars never stop begging because the need never goes away. I have talked to many people in fundraising and they all have such stories to tell. Charity's clients are the reason this work is like no other. You will get involved with people in a very real way.

Chapter 5 Meetings

"When shall we three meet again In thunder, lightning, or in rain?"

Macbeth (First Witch act I, i)

William Shakespeare (English playwright)

I attend many meetings. The non-profit world seems to be even more meeting prone than regular business. In part, that is because in the for-profit world, you are told what to do and expected to do it. In the non-profit world, you are often getting work done by volunteers and they are entitled to a degree of input and ownership of a task. Also, charities generally have more limited resources, so much discussion is involved in getting things and services donated that the for-profit world just goes out and buys as a matter of routine.

There are other reasons for the number of meetings, and it is dangerous to generalize and say all non-profits have more meetings than regular business, but the generality has some validity. Anyway, I go to a lot of meetings.

The need for meetings is one of the difficulties facing charities in recruiting volunteers to be on committees. As I have mentioned before, people do not want to commit their time to regularly scheduled meetings.

Another constant problem with meetings is finding a mutually agreeable time and location. Issues of where everyone is at a particular time of day, travel time, parking and the availability of the meeting space all have to be juggled.

If we hold breakfast meetings we interfere with those who have school age children. Often your meeting attendees are volunteers with regular jobs whose business may also like to hold early morning meetings. Lunch adds travel time in the middle of the day and lower level employees generally do not have the freedom to regularly take a two hour break in the middle of the day. And all meetings at meal times involve dealing with food, while meeting. The committee may not want mustard stains on the artwork they need to approve.

Meetings in the evening have a three-fold problem. First, one has the issue of older committee members and night driving. Second, people get home in the evening and do not want to go back out. They are tired and this is often the time for their families or their social life. Finally, evening meetings are the worst for dragging on. At breakfast or lunch, people have places to go and will leave early, if you do not watch the time carefully and move the meeting along in a rapid manner. At night, people are more likely to socialize and joke and the meetings can run on much longer than they need to.

A few years ago I and several other professional beggars were discussing when could a meeting be called that would generate the fewest conflicts. With all the factors of people's jobs, family, vacation and other obligations we agreed that the best time for a meeting was nine o'clock in the morning on New Year's Day.

We reasoned that it is a holiday that almost everyone has off and traditionally people are home sleeping off the night before. It is not a day associated with big family activities, dining out or picnics like Thanksgiving, Christmas or Labor Day. People may watch football in the afternoon but the morning is clear. We decided that the committee members might be hung over but could attend. Ironically, we also agreed that none of us had the nerve to schedule such a meeting.

I know these scheduling problems can be handled but I am not sure the cure is really a cure. First, the chair can run a tight businesslike meeting that requires written reports submitted prior to the meeting, and careful time controls on questions. Businesses often run meetings like that. However, most charities do not enjoy the luxury of tight control of their volunteers. If we try to establish it, we may get lots of resignations and little likelihood of recruiting new volunteers. Such total self discipline and dedication, while very admirable, is not so common as to keep the charities in America staffed with anywhere near the needed number of volunteers. We must work with what we can get. There are not enough Trappist monks to go around.

A partial solution to the time issue is the conference call. This does not remove the demands of the meeting time but does remove travel barriers. However, conference calls are not conducive to the free exchange of ideas or creation of a sense of membership so necessary in a strong, productive committee. This is even worse if the members do not already know each other fairly well. Conference calls are not a complete answer to the problem of turning individuals into a cooperative, productive group.

A sense of membership is important for a committee to be productive. Meetings may be long, boring, frustrating and hard to manage, but that does not make them a bad thing. Drawing people together to do good for others is always valuable in itself. Communion and communication both come from the same base word. Sharing of oneself with others is a basic human need and a basic part of charity.

Our modern communication system has done as much to isolate us as to bring us together. You can observe this in restaurants when two people sitting together and one is talking on a cell phone. The person not on the phone generally looks so isolated. Their companion has chosen to converse with someone who is not there rather than with them. Generally we apologize when we get off the phone after such a call because we realize it is a form of rejection of our companion, yet taking such calls has become the norm rather than the exception. We see constant news stories about the fact that Internet chat rooms can be dangerous for young people because the friend they meet on the Internet can turn out to be not another child but a pedophile. This can happen because we are not communicating with identifiable people on the Internet but with created disguised personalities. We are constantly warned about giving out personal information on the Internet because we can not always know who we are talking to. We use code names and passwords because the Internet is often not about communication with real people but with phantom created personalities. Cell phones and the Internet are examples of our new rapid communication but we are still often isolated from open honest communication with other people.

Charities, unlike businesses, are about love not profit. To maintain a regular flow of personal interaction, directed at doing good, is as important as the good itself. It may not seem like the Lord's Supper to sit around a table eating pizza and arguing about the budget for the fundraiser next month but look again. My understanding is that God will take us as he can get us. And he can get us to try to do for others as we would have done to us.

Chapter 6 The Face of Christ

"But when thou doest alms, let not thy left hand know what thy right hand doeth: That thine alms may be in secret: and thy Father which seeth in secret himself shall reward thee openly."

The Bible; Matthew 6:3-4

Much is written about why people support charities, and much is written in fund raising publications, such as Contributions Magazine or The NonProfit Times, about keeping donor's support. However, the most amazing and wonderful factor in much of charitable support is something that cannot be changed, or improved or even created. This is the direct and tangible presence of God.

For a person of faith, God is as present in a hospital ward as in a synagogue, as close to us in a homeless shelter as in a church, and as vital in a classroom as in a mosque. Many of the older hospitals in Europe and America bear the names of Saints or the names of the religious denominations that started them. Jews have practiced charity to strangers and foreigners as directed by the Torah since the time of Moses. The great universities of Islam were built by people devoted to God. It is not that the faithful expect to have what people would call spiritual experiences in these places. One has very human experiences, with extremely real people including people who are ignorant, sick, poor, crippled, lost, angry, insane and even dangerous. How the faithful react to these people is a clear measure of how clearly they see them, as God's most beloved creation and reflections of themselves. I will illustrate with the following example.

Occasionally groups of youth volunteer where I work. I take them around and explain what we do, and then they go to work. Often during the tour, or in a group discussion afterward, the question arises as to why this place even exists. I tell them this is a class in facial identification. I ask them, "What does Jesus Christ look like?" They will hem and haw for a while, and then one or two will say that the Bible does not give a description of Christ. I respond, "I can tell you exactly what Jesus looks like." I then point to one of them and say, "that's him, that's Jesus all right!" This generally produces a gasp and laughter, especially if I point to a girl. I will then quickly point to another face and say, "there, he looks just like him."

I will quickly do this two or three more times. My statement generally embarrasses the people I point to, and shocks and confuses the others, but they are all paying attention now. I explain that charities like this one exist so they can get used to seeing the wide variety of the face of Christ. I tell them that it will often be difficult to see Christ in others. I will point out that the face can be horribly distorted, but that it is still always there. I close by explaining to them that if they become proficient at spotting Christ on earth, they will have no difficulty finding him in Heaven. If however, they loose sight if Christ in the faces of the world, than how "at home" will they feel in heaven and how alien will Christ be?

For everyone involved with a charity, something touches him or her. It may be nothing more than stepping into a day care and receiving the warm loving embrace of a three year old that happens to be of a different race or the shock and horror that fills them as they hear a homeless mother relate the nightmarish circumstances that have brought her to the agency. They may not realize something has changed them, and if they do it may seem very mundane. Most of God's glorious triumphs are mundane in appearance. The birth of Jesus in a stable could not have looked very impressive. For the volunteer, the experience might be the sincerity in the voice of the person who asks them to help, the slight twinge of shame they feel over their own undeserved prosperity, or the warmth they get from a simple accomplishment that does real good. But often it is so intangible you cannot identify it.

The fact that a person can make a strong commitment to a charity does not mean charity work is always a happy experience. The longer one is involved with a charity the more they are aware of the fact that they are not a plaster saint, but a human dealing with humans. Anyone can get tired, frustrated and sometimes burnt out. That too is very human and there is nothing unusual about it. It is part of humanity. Even in the holiest of places, people are people. They can be lazy, slow and unproductive. A newsman wanting a statistic for a story he was writing asked Pope John the XXIII how many people worked in the Vatican. His Holiness' reply was, "oh about half of them."

As someone who works in a charity, I see donors and volunteers become frustrated and unhappy over decisions made by the charity, yet many of them continue their aid, year after year. This dedication to the charity is more than the fact that we run a reasonably good program. People commit their lives to charity all the time. They give, they work, and they care. They may never see the work completed; yet they stay, and generally stay joyfully. The places may not be new or clean, they may have clients who are difficult or even dangerous, and they may be working on a cause that can sometimes seem hopeless. Nevertheless, there is something that holds the donors and volunteers to the charity. With all its problems, it is still an aspect of Heaven on Earth. After all is not a place of care and love without reservation and without end what we hope Heaven is like? Any small effort to offer this to others and the joy we feel by doing it is moving us in the direction of bringing Heaven here.

Chapter 7 When to Ask

"It is difficult to live in the present, ridiculous to live in the future, and impossible to live in the past. Nothing is as far away as one minute ago."
Jim Bishop (journalist and author)

If you do much fishing then you are aware of the "couple of weeks ago" syndrome. Whenever you show up at a fishing spot, you will generally ask the locals how the fishing is. More often than not the reply is, "they were really biting a couple of weeks ago. They don't seem to be biting now." Weekend fishermen the world over have heard this response all the time. Fishing was always better "a couple of weeks ago" no matter when you show up.

When fundraisers talk shop, the issue of the best time of year to ask for money comes up. Many articles have been written and many lectures given on this topic. Often as not, I can count on the lecturer to give a very glowing, positive recommendation while some of my associates sitting near me may make a different comment on the time of year being discussed. Let me illustrate.

The speaker will say that right after the first of the year is a good time to ask, because people are making New Year's resolutions and they have a new budget to spend. My associates will point out that everyone is paying Christmas bills and has no money then.

Praise of early spring as a good time to ask is often tied to the optimism people experience due to the weather warming and plants turning green. Doubters point out the downside that donors are getting ready to pay their taxes, the financial blow of which cuts off interest in giving.

Late spring is sometimes recommended for fundraising events such as golf tournaments, marathons and outdoor parties.

Some of my peers will point out that this is true, but it is also the time of graduations and weddings, and people's calendars get booked up. In addition they have to buy expensive wedding or graduation gifts.

Summer is generally frowned upon as a time to raise money because people are away in the summer. For myself I have generally raised as much money in June, July and August as in other three-month periods. That may be because we have traditionally had both a major special event and our annual appeal in this period.

Fall is very popular as a time to fundraise. In many areas, the local United Way will also have its drive. This means that if an agency receives United Way funding, as ours does, they are asked by united Way not to do any fundraising of their own during the period, concentrating instead on helping the United Way campaign. For non-United Way charities this would seem to leave an open playing field yet, many fundraisers have told me that the heavy press from United Way, plus the fact that all the non agencies target this period, makes the season very cluttered. Besides, people have to send their kids back to school in this period and that can be a huge budget buster.

Finally, we come to the Holiday season. This is traditionally recognized as the best time to ask. Everyone is in a giving mood. Gratitude for one's good fortune and concern for others ill fortune is strong. But as usual there is a counter argument. Everyone is busy, everyone is stressed and every charity in the world is pestering people for money.

Thus, the definitive answer as to the best time to raise money is "never". It is best just to go ahead and ask. There is no right time except that now is always the best time. If a charity's need is now, it had better ask now, and if it doesn't have a need it is a very unusual charity.

Shortly after I started working at the agency I set up an annual appeal mailing in August. Of course, several of my fellow beggars pointed out to me that August was just about the worst time in the year to ask. I had picked August, not to be contrary, but because it was the only time in our year's calendar of fundraising with an opening. Over the years we have raised several hundred thousand dollars. This is not an endorsement of August as a great time to raise money. We went with what met the agency's needs best, as near as we could tell. This is not science and one often just has to feel one's way along.

So, if you are made responsible for raising money, pick the days on the calendar that will work best for your program and get to asking. The only day that is a real bad choice is February 30th!

Chapter 8 Staff and Volunteers

"To have a right to do a thing is not at all the same as to be right in doing it."

G. K. Chesterton (English writer)

I beg for a living and I get paid for my work. I am not a volunteer just trying to help others. So do I have any claim to charity having anything to do with me? Is it just a matter of proximity? I work for an organization that does good, and I am in constant contact with charitable people, but how is my employment related to my civic responsibility?

Consider, if someone has a minor job with a tobacco company, or a major polluter, or one where the officers are corrupt, does that person bear blame for what his bosses do? After all, an employee may have a family to support, and jobs are hard to come by. Is it fair to say they are guilty by association? The laws concerning employee responsibility says "no" and we Americans live by the law, because in America we control the law.

However, God has a different attitude, and sins of omission get people into trouble just as fast as sins of commission. In the story of the Good Samaritan (Luke 10:29) Jesus makes the Levite and the Pharisee, who passed by the wounded man, look bad even though they were not the ones who robbed him and beat him. While their guilt is less than the actual robbers they still have some. Even non Christians generally acknowledge that it seems heartless for leaders of the religious community to pass by someone in need without taking any action, even if it meant the possibility they might be made ritually unclean by touching a dead body. Only the Samaritan, who stops and helps, is acknowledged by those hearing Jesus tell the story as being a good neighbor. With this story in mind, is my job an act of charity?

I don't really think so. The people who volunteer their time or their money are the good guys in my story. If I want to be the Good Samaritan I have to do it on my own time. Nights, weekends, vacations, and the like are the times for me and all good beggars to do their bit for the world. We cannot count a job we are paid for as community service.

For the beggar, on the job performance gets judged on the issue of good work, versus good works. Good works are what the donors do. We must do good work, by which I mean good quality work. This is an issue often overlooked in modern America, but doing your best matters. Your best efforts may not be perfect, but they still should be your best. As beggars for the welfare of the world, our work is more important than in some other positions. After all, if you do poor work for a corporate or political thief; all you do is damage his ability to steal more. If you do poor quality work for a charity you are directly responsible for the resources of the donors, failing to help solve the problem. This is a gigantic responsibility. The weight of it can be more than anyone in the profession wants to think about but it is there.

I remember once that a young lady once requested my advice about asking for a raise. She had been working for a charity for about four years and was finding it difficult to make ends meet on her salary. She was reluctant to ask her boss for a raise because the charity needed all the money it could gather to help its clients. She was wondering if she should get out of charity work rather than further burden the place where she worked. I asked her to consider a scenario where if she was responsible for passing out raises. If she observed someone else doing her job and accomplishing what she was accomplishing would she give that person a raise? She said that she would. I recommended she ask for the raise and let her boss decide if increasing her pay was a wise use of the charity's resources. I pointed out that she clearly cared about the charity and was doing a good job. If the charity paid her enough to enable her to pay her bills she would continue to provide the charity with outstanding work. If she left, she could not guarantee the agency would find someone else with the same degree of ability and dedication. She agreed to follow my advice and let her boss decide if she deserved the raise. She received the raise and assurances from her boss and several members of the charity's board that her work was excellent and she was much valued. She is still working there today and doing a great job.

On the whole, I have observed that fundraisers are in their line of work for more than the paycheck. I have met many of them over the years, and they tend to work hard and accomplish much with limited resources. Certainly, there are exceptions, and even the best can burn out, but on the whole they are brave, patient, loyal and energetic. Many of them volunteer to sit on boards, teach classes, and serve as advisers to charities that cannot afford full time development staffs. They give their time and their knowledge freely to help others. These people are what make this line of work so much fun.

Shortly after I started my job the federal government announced plans to reduce the number of people on welfare. Our agency realized this meant we would have an increasing number of people in the area needing jobs, and in many cases these would be people with no education or marketable skills that would often be responsible for the care of others in their household. Such people need jobs with flexible hours and little or no formal training. These people were unlikely to own or be able to afford transportation so jobs in the nearby area would be a major part of the solution.

We had a full time social worker who was concerned with this issue and felt he saw a way to help. At the time this man was responsible for all clients who walked in off the street. He also ran our clothing thrift shop, our food pantry and our Christmas gift program. In other words, he had a full-time job, no help and was very busy. In his spare time he was an expert on the welfare-to-work issue who was routinely contacted by the state legislature members and their staffs for input. His personal life included a wife, a teenaged daughter and his calling as a clergyman in a local church. As I said he was very busy.

He reasoned that with the number of elderly in the area increasing, we could set up a program to hire clients needing work to go into the homes of elderly area residents to provide housekeeping services for them. The jobs would have flexible hours, require little or no training and would be primarily in the local neighborhood. In addition, it would allow us to provide care for our clients who due to age or infirmity could no longer come to the agency for help. Finally, as the concept developed, he also realized he could use elderly clients in the area to act as companions to the homebound elderly. This would allow our more mobile clients to volunteer in the neighborhood and feel useful as they helped their neighbors who were lonely and needed a regular visitor. It was a perfect win- win situation. There was only one problem.

The problem was money. Such a program needs staff to supervise it and schedule visits. The federal government was willing to pay for such services to the elderly and others through the Medicaid and Medicare programs. However, the whole thing would have to be put together, up and running, before such money would start to make the program self sufficient. It was going to require a lot of money up front to put the thing into action and additional money to cover expenses until the program could prove self sufficient. Fortunately, such money was theoretically available through a grant from the government and help from the local United Way.

The head of the agency thought the idea sounded good but there was no staff available to put it into action and no money either. The social worker was basically on his own. He had to develop a complete business plan, write grant applications to the government and United Way, and set the entire program up from scratch. He also had to continue doing his regular job. So that is precisely what he did.

If you are not familiar with the process of writing a grant to the federal government let me assure you it is a complex one. This book is not as thick as all the paperwork required. The IRS long tax return is small potatoes in comparison. Also, when you are done, Uncle Sam is perfectly willing to send it back and tell you to do it over again in a different way. The entire process went on over a year. The social worker exploded in understandable frustration more than once during this period. After all, he was single handedly meeting the demands of government bureaucrats to get the grant and doing his regular job at the same time.

Finally the process was done and the programs were in place and funded. The social worker was worn down and soon left the agency, but he had gotten the whole thing started and started well. I see him every now and then and he is just as active as ever. He is a full time pastor, involved with several causes and an active force in the church's policies at the conference level. A man still filled with energy and dedication that I hold in great respect and awe. When he left the agency, it took three full time staff to replace him.

This is an example of doing good quality work. His efforts made a real difference in the lives of the people he was trying to help. This kind of dedication and creativity is often found in charities. Dedicated people, who in the world of wealth and power, are often as socially unacceptable as Samaritans were in Jesus' time. Yet when one is in trouble or need these "Good Samaritans" are the type of people one needs more than any other.

Chapter 9 Endowment

"The future belongs to those who prepare for it today."
Malcolm X (social activist)

An important aspect of begging is endowment, by which I mean a permanent endowment. An endowment is a gift and a permanent endowment is a gift that keeps on giving over time.

Let me explain. An endowment is a gift of money, property, stocks, bonds or other valuables. The deal is that the donor says you can't spend the money. You can only spend the interest or revenue generated by the gift. The principal (the gift itself) must stay in place to generate more interest for next year and so on and so on, thus the permanent part of the deal.

Endowments are popular with institutions because there is the promise of money being always available. In good years or bad, the interest on the endowment will be there and a charity can do some long-term budget planning safely. The charity has a nest egg it can depend on.

Donors like endowments as well. If the donor thinks a charity are a fine institution and is doing good work, their endowment insures this good work will continue long into the future. Three years down the road an irresponsible new president or unwise new board of directors can't say, "Well let's just spend all of this money right now and not worry about the future." The law says that if you accept the gift you have to live with whatever strings the donor attached to it which includes only spending the interest. The donor can see to it that the fund is named after them or someone they want remembered. That way every year the George Jones endowment will pay to send a deserving child to camp, a student to school, or whatever cause the family of George Jones wanted to assist.

You may notice I do not say "forever", and frankly I do not like the term "permanent endowment". There is a down side to all this but in most cases it will not matter until long after everyone involved is dead. The reality is that there is no such thing as "permanent". The institution one endows may close, or the cause one wishes to help may disappear. Not long ago there were a number of court cases to redirect endowments set up to fund orphanages. The changes in the way most orphaned or abandoned children are handled by the legal system have seen to it that most orphanages are gone now. Adoption and foster care have, to a large degree, ended these institutions. However, many orphanages had been endowed and the courts had to decide how to reallocate the money. This was no small issue because the money must go to some other type of child assistance or to the heirs of the person who set up the endowment.

Inflation will also finally end many endowments. Three hundred years ago, if someone set up a scholarship to send young men to college, $10,000 created a big endowment. Today, the paperwork alone will cost much of the few hundred dollars the interest would generate. These days, $500 will not send you to college for two days, much less four years. Nothing on this earth is forever.

Most institutions have a rule that if the overhead on a gift gets to be burdensome they may invade the principle until it is exhausted. I remember when we got the last check on an endowment set up in the late 1800s. The bank that was administering it closed it down and dispersed what was left. This frequently happens to smaller endowments. If immortality is a donor's motivation than they must recognize that the longer the immortality wanted the more money needed in the pot to start.

Any gift with strings attached can have problems. As situations change, those strings can lead to some interesting ways of using the money while still keeping true to the donor's intent. A rural church I once visited was left a large endowment by a lady who had taught one of the Sunday school classes for many years. The endowment was to be spent only for the betterment of that one Sunday school class. As time passed and the church needed money for various renovations and repairs, a very interesting thing began to happen. Each year that Sunday school class needed a "new improved room". So a room in the church would be refurbished and the class would move in. The next year they would move to another room that would need fixing. That one class wandered all over the church. They even met in the kitchen and the sanctuary before it was all over. Finally the church decided it could not go on with this farce and went to court, at considerable expense, to get the terms of the endowment altered.

In spite of the problems I have mentioned, I recommend endowment. However, if you want to keep an institution "doing good work" it is best not tie its hands too tightly.

Finally, if you want to keep the memory of your dear departed mother alive for generations to come, plan on a seven or eight figure gift. Anything less will be gone before your grandchildren are.

Chapter 10 The Show Must Go On

"Every man is guilty of all the good he did not do."

Voltaire (French philosopher)

I was the first full-time development staff person my agency had employed. Before my arrival the head of the agency had done the fundraising along with all the other responsibilities of running the agency. The agency had grown steadily under his leadership and now needed a full time fundraiser. As the first, I had both the opportunity and responsibility of taking the agency's fundraising in new directions. This was both exciting and frightening. It was wonderful to be creative and break new ground yet I was aware that the agency was depending on me to make sure the new ground I was moving into would bring in enough money to insure the agency's survival and continued growth. I had enough experience with new business ventures to know how easily they could get into trouble and fail. I understood my job was to increase agency revenue not agency expenses and I wanted my projects to be a series of shining successes not dark failures. Unfortunately, my first really big project was not a shining success and was almost a dark failure. Let me tell you about it.

The agency board and staff knew that the agency needed greater public awareness of its existence and its fine work and felt it suffered from a lack of recognition. I understood that greater exposure would aid in two ways. First, it would gain additional supporters as they heard of the agency and its wonderful community work. Second, publicity would inspire and invigorate present supporters when they saw how popular and respected their favorite charity was. This should result in more support from them. The board's development committee decided that an unusually large public fundraiser would gain publicity and bring a large sum of money from the event itself. I began researching various special events.

One truth about special events is that the bigger they are, the more time, manpower and money required. Several years before, the agency had begun an annual craft auction. This event occurred in a local church where one to two hundred people ate dinner and bid on donated crafts or baked goods. This event was the agency's biggest fundraiser and brought in five to ten thousand dollars. I was trying to raise ten or twenty times that amount with my new event.

I had the name of a famous opera singer whose family was connected to the agency. I contacted this person to see if she would be willing to donate a performance. She agreed and the development committee set about planning the event. I worked out an agreement on a date for the concert that was over a year in the future. I discovered as the complexity of this event grew that a year could rush by with the speed of a bullet.

The committee had to book an affordable location that met our performer's needs. I secured the concert hall of the city's major symphony which seated several thousand people and had wonderful acoustics. All I had to do was fill it with paying customers.

I should point out that with a concert, play or other event where one has an audience the money is made from the sale of the tickets. One may gather some extra revenue from souvenirs or refreshments but generally the profit comes from ticket sales. The price for the tickets depends on a number of factors including the popularity of the performer, and the charity, and the concert expenses. Of course, the ideal situation is to sell all tickets at the highest price possible. If one prices the tickets too low, they may sell out the hall but not cover expenses. If one prices the tickets too high, they will only sell them to people who are devoted to the performer or the charity and that may not fill the hall.

As the date grew closer my boss (the head of the agency) and the members of the board of directors became increasingly alarmed. We had one board member who had always been skeptical of the agency's ability to handle such a large event. More and more board members were voicing concerns. They were signing contract after contract for large sums of money to put on a concert that would have to come out of the agency's operating budget if things went badly. One of the first expenses was the rental of the concert hall and in this case it amounted to several thousand dollars. I had decided on a reasonable ticket price and had even worked out a formula as to how much money the agency would make if I sold all the tickets or half the tickets or only a third of the tickets. At the same time the formula only worked if I controlled expenses. That was something that proved easier said than done.

With any charity event one goal of the beggar is to get as many expense items as possible donated. Again, in an ideal situation everything is donated and all the money raised goes to the charity. Special events rarely meet this ideal. Our star was donating her time and several advertisers were donating publicity but there was much I had to pay for. I had to pay for the concert hall, the staff needed to put on the show and the rehearsals, food and lodging for the other performers and musicians brought to town for the show, publicity, printing, legal fees, insurance and much more. Each day the concert drew closer and each day the expenses grew higher. Then the tickets went on sale.

For months I had been assuring the board, my boss, the development committee and everyone else that this concert could work if enough people came. The event had grown larger and larger due to many factors and I realized it might be a disaster, but with the signing of each contract and the payment of each non-refundable deposit, it became increasingly impossible to get out without a huge financial loss. So on we plunged hoping to sell enough tickets to save us from disaster. When the first reports of how ticket sales were going came in I thought I was going to be sick. The concert was only a couple of weeks away and tickets were not moving.

For the next two weeks my boss and I ran to every individual and group we could, begging people to come to the show. Our staff and volunteers were phoning people day and night. Slowly the tickets sold and at last it was concert night.

We had managed to assemble the largest crowd ever of our supporters. There were people from all over the city who wanted to see our star. Unfortunately, it still was not enough. The hall was more than half empty.

The concert was wonderful and everyone but me had a great time. People crowded back stage to thank our star and congratulated my boss and me on a great fundraiser. I personally felt like crawling into a hole. I felt bad for our star who had wanted to help us, for our board and volunteers who had been so hopeful, and for myself because I had not delivered the goods.

In the aftermath, my boss analyzed the expenses and the revenue and found that we could legitimately argue that we had more or less broken even. This was better than the disaster we had been facing two weeks before, but it was a long way from the huge monetary windfall we had anticipated a year before. I feared I was going to be fired. My boss supported his staff but if the board wanted a scapegoat I was the logical target. When the board met a few days latter I attended as I always did. As I mentioned, there was one member of the board who had been skeptical of this event from the beginning. He had expressed reservations at each of the meetings when it became clear that the concert was more expensive than anticipated. He and his family had been there the night of the show so he knew the size of the audience. If anyone could legitimately say "I told you so" this was the person. After my report there were one or two questions and this board member raised his hand to speak. I was stunned as he said that no blame for the concert's failure to raise money should go to either me or my boss. He said the board, including him, had approved this project and the board should shoulder the responsibility for it. He expressed his opinion that this was a worthwhile learning experience and had benefited the agency in many ways. Finally, he stated that he hoped the board would not be discouraged by this event but would continue to have the development department try new ideas and keep moving forward. The board gave his words a loud vote of support and I left the meeting feeling ten feet tall.

I offer this story as an example of the fact that people who work for charities are only human. They have to learn on the job and they make mistakes. If you are aware that the staff at your favorite charity is doing something wrong, it is completely appropriate for you to say something about it.

Please, just show some understanding and patience when you do. You'll be appreciated.

Chapter 11 Dead Dead Dead

"It's not your salary that makes you rich; it's your spending habits."

Charles A. Jaffe (financial columnist)

"There are no pockets in shrouds." "You can't take it with you." "No corpse ever complained about the quality of his funeral." "You cannot slander the dead." All these expressions emphasize that what is important in this life will not matter in the next. They also point out that your power in this world stops when you die. At death you loose your money and your rights. People try to dodge these facts all the time. They want to have some say about what was theirs when they were alive. However, the old adage "If you want something done right do it yourself" is hard to practice after death. The will, the trust, the power of attorney and all such legal terms, are about trying to keep control over what you can no longer own.

In charity work we are very interested in wills as people often leave money to charities. There are many of reasons for this situation. Often, those making such bequests did not have much money and they needed what they had to live on. People's homes and farms, often come to charities when the owner no longer needs a place to live or land to work. Money sometimes comes for the same reason. When someone is retired on a fixed income, they may worry about outliving their money. Once they die, it is not necessary to maintain that nest egg. If they do not have children or if their relationship with their children is very good or very bad, a charity can wind up with some or all of the estate.

Concerning the children, I said very good or very bad. If it is very bad, they won't want to leave their children anything and so act accordingly. However, the law will often stop parents from punishing their children too much, and many a charity has found itself in a big lawsuit when the children challenge the will. Of course the more common situation is that the parents have a good relationship with the children. These parents expect their adult children to be self-sufficient and have been open with the children about their desire to help a charity. There is rarely trouble about the will in such a case.

A popular saying with a number of wise parents these days goes "I want to give my children enough for them to do anything but not so much that they can do nothing." Such people often set up charitable foundations or trusts and involve the children in the giving process early on. This speaks of a mature and open relationship, which will result in support for the charity continuing from generation to generation. However, people can give money for the "wrong" reasons and I need to touch on that.

A Jewish saying states "What you give to charity in health is gold, in sickness is silver, and after death is lead." One aspect of this saying touches on the issue of sacrifice. In the Judeo-

Christian world sacrifice is an important part of true charity. If you only give after your death, you are giving what has become valueless to you. You have made no sacrifice at all. I am reminded of a joke about two drunks that illustrates this point.

One drunk was dying and asked his friend to do him a favor. "Anything old friend, just name it", replied the second drunk. "I have kept a bottle of very expensive whiskey for many years. I want you to pour it over my grave," said the first. "Of course!" said the second drunk "but can I filter it through my kidneys first?"

If by giving people are trying to buy immortality or their way into heaven, they are wasting their time. In the Middle Ages, people bought prayers to get out of purgatory. Now many people want to make up for in death what they had no interest in during life. While it does help charity I must point out that the donor is being foolish. If someone has spent their life looking down on others as trash, that individual is foolish to think that eternal life will be a private affair involving only a few acceptable associates. An eternal life that includes many people one has a bias against is the only one to reasonably expect. God has not promised to put up a little special Heaven just for the social elite. All major religions agree that your brother is your brother, like it or not, and all mankind is your brother. A love of Heaven, like beer, is an acquired taste and people have to learn to appreciate certain aspects of it, such as loving others, while they are alive. Otherwise, it is not that they will be kicked out; they will walk out and seek a place where they get the attention they think they deserve. That place has the traditional name of Hell but nobody there calls it that. The great C.S. Lewis wrote a wonderful book called The Great Divorce, which describes Heaven and Hell as places people pick, and how many will reject Heaven even when it is offered after death.

Now do not misunderstand my position. I am not talking about tainted money. As a matter of fact, there is no such thing as "tainted" money. Charities spend money to do good, whatever its source. The Roman emperor Diocletian was criticized by his son Titus for taking revenue money from a tax on the city toilets. The emperor's response was, "money doesn't stink." A rose will grow fine in a dung heap and still smell sweet. A charity can feed the poor with a pirate's money as easily as a saint's. The difference is in what good the donation is doing the donor. There can be a difference, and sometimes the charity's beggar has the responsibility of the donor's welfare to consider as well as the beneficiary. That can be tough.

The beggar might have donors who wanted to insure their name in history. The beggar cannot promise to deliver that. If a donor wants to fund medical research, the beggar cannot be sure his institution will make the breakthrough that allows the donor to be remembered as the person who financed the cure for cancer, heart disease, or even hang nails. The beggar will not be doing right by the donors, and the name of the charity may become famous for being the biggest liars in town. As for a name carved deep on a big new building, such buildings may be remodeled, demolished, or burn down. The name will disappear with the building. In many older cities, you will see buildings with the company name of the former owner still carved over the door. But now there is a big bright new sign to say who the new owner is, and the old name is worn and ghostly. The beggar can promise a name on something, but must not promise it to remain there forever. Nothing is forever, and the donor may wake up and realize this and also realize the beggar is a fool, a cheat, or maybe both. The beggars are the custodians of the donor's good will and must not betray that trust. The development department is often the only regular contact a donor will have with a charity. The other departments do the work of the charity but the people in the development department are responsible for maintaining contact with the donor and are generally the people most likely to be aware of the donor's needs and wishes. If the development department does not make the charity's decision makers aware of the donor's needs and wishes, and the donor aware of the charities limitations in meeting those needs and wishes, no one else will.

I want to come back to the issue of sacrifice. If you do not believe in God, or you do not believe what most major religions say of him, you may find the issue of sacrifice meaningless. However, for the faithful we are back to the word charity. Charity is love and love is expressed through sacrifice. If parents did not sacrifice time, effort, and money to feed, shelter, and protect their child, no child would live. A child cannot survive on its own and it cannot, and will not, payback all that is done for it. You can tell someone you love them but if you refuse to be inconvenienced, or make any effort to help, they will not believe your words of love.

Lover's language is full of the exuberance or giving. "I want to give you the moon and stars." Doing and giving for the beloved is normal. In a mature married relationship, each partner understands that, as a couple, each must sacrifice part of themselves to make their partnership strong. There is no other way it can grow and prosper. Sacrifice is a measure of love. In the Bible story of the Widow's Mite, Jesus Christ makes his attitude very clear when he points out the poor widow putting two small coins into the offering after the rich have made their large gifts. They have given out of wealth but she has given all she has. Jesus teaches that the degree of sacrifice is the measure of the gift, not the amount. (Luke 21:1-4)

Now again this puts a strain on the beggar. The beggar knows that a large gift buys more for the charity, but to brush off the small gifts of one who gives sacrificially is an easy way to poison one's own heart. These are the moments the beggar gets to see God in the world, and would be a great fool to miss them because of the blinding glitter of gold. To bear conscious witness to the gift of the widow's mite may very well be the only job-related question a beggar is asked about on judgment day. The beggar should want that memory to be clear and bright, and the telling of it a tale of glory and wonder.

Chapter 12 Time

"All my possessions for a moment of time."
Queen Elizabeth I of England (at her death)

The director of my agency has announced his retirement after twenty-seven years. That is a long time. Yet staff tends to stay at our agency a long time. While there is only one person in over one hundred full and part time staff who has been there longer than the director several have been here twenty years or more. I have just started my twelfth year here and I am still one of the new kids and I still feel sort of new. Reflecting on this makes me realize that in spite of my length of employment I feel that my time here has gone by very quickly.

Do you remember when you were a child how long it took to get through a year? The holidays seemed ages away when school started up and even a week seemed to drag on forever. Now I routinely start laying out calendar dates for events one and even two years in advance with a feeling I may not have enough time to get everything ready. I find that years blur together and months go by like lightning especially with a deadline looming.

I understand that part of this feeling of time running faster is because in the days of grade school each year was completely different. One generally started the fall with a different teacher, different classroom and different subjects to study. At work a person will generally be with the same people doing the same job each year and if it changes dramatically it will not do so by the calendar. I find my old school experiences cause me to think of fall rather than January as the beginning of a New Year.

I am keenly aware that time is changeable, flowing, and personal. All the artificial clockwork measurements in the world have not altered this reality. Time spent visiting with an old friend, watching a sunset or reading a good book stands still, while time in the dentist chair moves very slowly and time races by when people are running late. Believe it or not, our feelings about time relate to charity. Let me explain.

For the most part, giving is about time. Employers pay employees for their time as much as their efforts or expertise. Hourly wage, billable hours and being on the clock are all phrases that describe the dollar value of time. Everyone knows that, "Time is money." When one donates to charities they are giving the fruits of their time as much as the fruits of their labor. A person is paid for their time and this money theirs to keep or give to others.

Of course, we can give our time directly. A volunteer gives their time, while collecting for their favorite charity door to door, or reading to a blind person, or giving blood. The volunteer is not paid and not forced to act. That is why using the term "volunteer" for people doing community service, as punishment for traffic violations or other misdemeanors, is ridiculous. They are not volunteers they are draftees. Their attitude toward the work shows the difference. Generally, they want to arrive late and leave early. They tend to work as slowly as possible and often complain about how slow the time goes.

Someone working off a traffic fine is no more a volunteer than someone paying taxes is a donor to the government. One may hear people say they help others by paying their taxes. But paying taxes is not charity it is legal and accepted coercion. We may argue as to how much we each need to pay in taxes, but the majority of us agree that individuals do not get to exempt themselves from paying. A tax is not a gift and a draftee is not a volunteer.

So often, volunteers can undervalue their gift of time. They will apologize for not doing more, say they do not have much money and can only act as a volunteer rather than a donor. Yet personal time commitment is one of the hardest things for a charity to get. "I don't want to be on a committee and attend meetings" is a common objection. "Do I have to show up? Can't I just send you a check?" is a more popular phrase now than ever before. Volunteers need to know that if they did not show up, the charity would have to hire and pay someone to replace them. Please understand I realize volunteers bring more than just a warm body to fill a slot. Creativity, dedication, enthusiasm and selflessness are just some of the positive traits common to volunteers.

Giving blood is one of the most interesting volunteer activities. I have been involved in blood drives, and am amazed that nothing else, including money, will substitute for blood. We must take time out of our busy day, to lie still, and experience a momentary pain in the arm. That is it. The human body produces extra blood, which healthy people can give with no danger to themselves. (The issue of contamination concerns the receiver not the giver.) Yet without this donation, of something we have in abundance, other people will literally die. Taking the time to give blood it is the whole issue. Rich or poor, strong or weak, we all have extra blood. In many ways it is the perfect donation.

As I said, my boss is retiring. Twenty-seven years is a long time. Or is it? I know for myself that I cannot remember the exact passage of the days that have occupied my work as a Development Director over the years. I can feel the weariness of age being more pronounced than it was twenty years ago but not the chronology of actions that happened with any great degree of exactitude. Nonetheless, time has passed for me and for others. In my boss's case it was clearly time well spent, for many people have been helped by this agency and it is both larger and in better financial health than when he started. Still, he is concerned with the present. Meetings to attend, reports to study, and decisions to be made are part of his regular day. That is as it should be because it is in the present, not the past or the future, that we connect with eternity.

Chapter 13 Sunday School

"The best test of your faith is when the collection plate comes around and the smallest you have is a twenty."
Milton Berle (comedian)

I taught 6th and 7th grade Sunday school for 12 years. One of my favorite lessons that worked well, with the kids, involved their coming to grips with the issue of the true worth of money, whether it was their master or servant, and the importance of giving.

This lesson worked particularly well in December when Christmas and the school holidays were coming, and the kids were restless. When I walked in the youngsters were often noisy and unruly. Instead of trying to calm them, I would loudly ask why they were excited. They would say that Christmas was coming. I would ask what was the most important thing about Christmas, and one of them would always yell, "Presents!" At this point they would expect me to disagree and say something about Jesus. However, I would always agree and shout," Yes, and what is the best present?" Again, I could count on lots of answers that had nothing to do with Jesus. Finally someone would shout, "Money" and I would loudly agree. By this time the class would be in a complete uproar.

I would march around chanting, "money, money, who wants money?" The kids would all hold up their hands and yell back "me, me". I would take out a twenty-dollar bill, and ask if everyone wanted some money. The shouts would be very loud and I would tear up the twenty, and give each child a piece. At this point the room got a lot quieter.

These were the children of reasonably affluent parents, and they knew that money had value, and you did not destroy it. They would look very puzzled and ask, with some annoyance, what I was doing. I pretended complete innocence, and answered, that they said they wanted money, and I had given them money. One of the children would then point out the obvious fact that they couldn't spend this money. I would then act angry and incredulous, and ask if they all wanted to spend the money. They quickly agreed, "Of course", they wanted to spend it. I then asked what they wanted to buy and would receive a long list of toys, games and entertainment items. I generally asked if they received such presents the previous Christmas. They would mention their favorite gifts from last year.

At this point, I picked on one child, who had proudly spoken of a gift. I asked about the color of the box the gift came in. In some confusion the child replied that the item was no longer in its box and the box was tossed last Christmas. I acted completely amazed, at this, and asked why he took a chance on damaging his precious gift by moving it from one storage box to another.

The child would state that it was not in a storage box, and I would look puzzled for a moment. I then turned on the child and asked if he had, by some act of madness, been playing with the toy. The child would say "yes", though not with quite the same self-assurance he had been using earlier.

I would then tell the class that while one of their number had gone insane, that I felt sure none of the others were actually "using" the gifts they had wanted for Christmas. They would then admit that they were all using their gifts. By this time things would be pretty quiet. These children were not stupid and they could smell a trap. They knew something was up, but they had not followed me completely.

I would then act as ridiculously pompous as possible and state that I was shocked to discover they were a bunch of dreadful liars. I would point out that they had assured me of their love of money, but when given some, they only wanted to spend it. They had said that they wanted to buy things, but then revealed they would use their things, rather than carefully preserving them, so their assurances of wanting things was also not true. I then told them that I could trust none of their responses because they kept lying to me.

I had better point out here that I got along pretty well with my classes. A close friend of mine had been co-teaching with me from the start, we knew each other's style and we generally had a third person to help. I never talked down to my students, I let the showoffs show off and they generally calmed down after a bit.

A child of eleven or twelve is just starting to be independent. They have discovered mom and dad are not all knowing, and this causes a degree of superficial arrogance. They bore easily and can disrupt a class in a matter of seconds, yet they are ready to do some serious thinking and they have a strong sense of justice. (Coincidentally, this is a good age to start them doing volunteer work, because they will care about the people they help, and may make such volunteering a lifelong activity.) If you give them a piece of real, deep, complex theology to look at, they will plunge right in. Transubstantiation, Free Will verses The Omniscience of God, Grace verses Works, and many others, are good grist for their mill.

The boys tend to be a bit behind the girls, in social skills, but will become avid Bible readers, if you point out the gory and gross parts. I had several parents disturbed and a few delighted because their eleven-year-old sons were avidly reading the book of Judges. Judges is as violent and blood soaked as an Arnold Schwarzenegger movie, but it is just as much a part of the Bible, as any other. So, they might be reading it for all the wrong reasons, but they were reading the

Bible. They will get around to some of the other books when the spirit moves them. My point is, in all this digression that my students have often thought me slightly crazy, but they were not afraid of me.

By this time, I had the complete attention of the class and they all wanted to know where this was leading. I asked why they played with their toys. The reply came back that it was fun. I then inquired if having fun was a good feeling. The class would indulge my obvious stupidity with a very condescending "yes, fun was a good feeling." It was time to enter the home stretch.

I asked each of them if they could remember doing something for someone that left them with a really good feeling. A feeling so strong they could still feel a bit of it now, as they remembered and described the event. They would reply with stories about helping a friend, doing something nice for mom, volunteering at the local homeless shelter, or patching up a dispute with a bratty sibling. I then pointed out that none of these strong feeling were about money but were about giving something of themselves.

I would then tell them that giving was what Christmas was all about. God gave himself to us and we become more Godlike when we give ourselves to others. I would suggest that they consider money only as a tool, not an end. I would remind them they had just proven this with their own responses. I would tell them that I had a good feeling about them and because I did, I had been perfectly willing to waste a twenty-dollar bill on them. I then wished them a very Merry Christmas. I told them to enjoy their gifts, especially if they got cash, for they were the masters of their possessions, rather than the possessions being the masters of them. I then declared class over.

They always left very quietly.

Chapter 14 Envy

"I am Envy. I cannot read and therefore wish all books burned."

Doctor Faustus

Christopher Marlowe (English playwright and poet)

I need to discuss envy. Greed and envy are the two negative personality traits most closely connected with money, and therefore play a major role in Beggarland. Greed blocks giving, more often than any other human trait. Greed is fairly straightforward, and I cannot do anywhere as good a job in describing it as Charles Dickens did in "A Christmas Carol". I like the old black and white film version with Alister Sym as Scrooge. There is a great scene early in the film where Scrooge is having dinner alone in a tavern. He asks the waiter for some more bread and the waiter replies that it will cost a penny. "No more bread, waiter", says Scrooge. Scrooge was so greedy he would not even spend money on himself! Greed is an important subject in fundraising and we will get to it, but right now let us talk about envy.

Envy or jealously is generally deemed a problem more for the have nots rather than the haves, but it is fascinating who claims to "have not". It is possible for one of the richest men in a country to spend all his time in envy of the few people ahead of him, and never have a moment of gratitude that he is better off then 99.99 % of his countrymen. In Snow White we have a classic case of envy where the queen is the most beautiful woman in the land until Snow White comes along. Upon learning this, the queen can think of nothing but destroying Snow White. The fact she is still more beautiful than all but one plus being queen gives her no satisfaction and in the end she destroys herself trying to kill Snow White.

It is important to understand that envy generally hides its face. People will admit to being gluttonous, greedy, arrogant or bad tempered. They may even brag about being lustful or lazy. However people do not like to admit to envy. If someone is accused of being jealous, they will often get angry and defensive. An admission of true envy may be an admission of inferiority, and that admission clashes with personal pride. In Christian history most of the serious theologians recognized pride (also known as arrogance, conceit, smugness, self-importance, egotism, vanity) as the most powerful and dangerous sin of all. We all have it, and it is anchored deep, so envy must disguise itself to avoid upsetting our pride.

Righteous indignation is often very close to envy but there is a difference. If I say, "He should not act like that" I may just be identifying a legitimate wrong. However, if I say, "If I had his power, or looks, or whatever I would never act as bad as him," then envy may be part of my evaluation. If I say to myself, "it is not fair that he has all that he has and I don't," then I am envious. If I see someone with money, power, beauty, strength or popularity, and I feel anger as I say, "they don't deserve it" than envy is behind the anger.

This matters in the beggar game because people can become envious of the recipients of charity. Some cute little poster child in a wheelchair will, sooner or later, produce the angry growl "I wish someone would push that kid's chair off a steep cliff". When asked to help the poor, people may respond, "The poor are lazy. They just sit around, getting a free ride, while I have to work". Yet none of the people who say this want to join the poor, in their "free ride", and will be very upset if their job disappears.

What are they jealous of? They don't want to be poor and they certainly don't want to be crippled. What is it they envy? The answer is they envy the charity. Remember, charity is love. We are all so hungry for love; it is almost impossible not to envy someone else we see receiving it. The public outpouring of charity for little Jimmy in his wheelchair, the hungry children in Africa, even the abandoned dog at the animal shelter, is burning acid on a love starved heart. The response may be a scream of pure jealousy.

People in the beggar game must never forget that their cause is not the only wound on the planet which needs fixing. The planet is filled with all sorts of people, with all sorts of heavy burdens. The number of people who receive all the love they need and want is very small. Envy is negative and blocks reason, but it often flows from a very real, common human condition of an empty heart. Beggars need not be critical of people who turn their backs or criticize begging. Such people may just not be able to stand the pain of seeing love flow elsewhere.

A few years back our local United Way offered my charity the chance to set up a table in a shopping mall as a way for us to offer information about our programs to the public and to encourage giving. Most people just walked by. A few people who recognized our name came by to say hello and wish us well and some asked about what sort of programs we had. One man came up to ask what I was doing. I started to explain about the different programs we had to help poor people get out of poverty and how United Way money supported us. He became surprisingly angry and demanded to know why he should help the poor. I replied that people helped for different reasons but he cut me off and told me that no one had ever helped him when he was growing up. He said he had dropped out of school early and worked very hard with no support or care from anyone all his life. He was not bragging about having pulled himself up by his own bootstraps but was deeply bitter about his past. I suggested that considering how hard things had been for him he might want to give to help someone else avoid such suffering. The idea seemed to strike him dumb. Shortly he recovered and said with finality, "until someone pays me back for all I went through, I won't help anyone". He left and I never saw him again.

Christians are supposed to understand the power of envy in people's lives. If they are being honest with themselves they see it in their own lives. The existence of envy is one reason Christians acknowledge their need for God's grace to help gain eternal life. Christians are also greedy, slothful, and vain, like everyone else. All of these failings will be cured by eternal love. But, until they are cured, we are all walking wounded in the world.

Chapter 15 Xmas

"Let's dance and sing and make good cheer,

For Christmas comes but once a year."

Sir George Alexander Macfarren (Scottish composer)

I am writing this during the last week of December. I generally take a few days off around Christmas. Most of the giving decisions have been made and it can be a rather unpleasant time in a development department if we came up short of our goal for the year. Year end financial jitters are brought on by a sort of last minute desperation, which can seize both management and board members. Everyone wants to end the year in the black, and will try to think of some way they can get more donations at the last minute. This is an emotional response rather than a fund raising strategy and automatically clears up on January 2. We will come back into the office, and realize that the business year is just a measuring tool, and the same bills are there as well as the same supporters who were there on December 31. We just start over, or in reality merely continue what we were doing all along. If we had a good year, the euphoria ends just as quickly as the depression in a bad year. I prefer to avoid the emotional roller coaster that kicks in about mid-December so I try to take a short vacation.

Most donors have decided how much they are going to give my agency, for any one year, by mid-December. They may wait to send the check until the last moment, but it is not because they forgot and suddenly realize they need to make their charitable contribution for the tax year before January 1. They may have any number of financial reasons to wait until the last minute, but not because the end of the year snuck up on them. After all, there is a large traditional reminder that December is the time of giving, and I do not mean Christmas.

The reminder is what I will refer to as, Xmas. Xmas is, economically speaking, the biggest sale in America. One third of all retail business is done during Xmas. Electric bills increase across the land from all the extra lights. An entire style of music used only in this season comes out of radios, store loud speakers and almost everywhere else. The post office is buried in Xmas cards and letters to the North Pole. To top it off, we are surrounded with images and replicas of an obscure historical figure that has been transformed to take on the image and power of God for many in our land _ Santa.

I understand that there is a difference between Xmas and Christmas. Christmas is a religious celebration, for Christians, which celebrates their Savior's birth and looks forward to his return. It is a 12 day long season in the church calendar, starting December 25 and ending January 5 (Twelfth Night). Xmas is a modern American season, which did not really become popular until the 20th century. It now starts right after Halloween and ends the first weekend after December 25, to cover the last of the post Xmas shopping. Along with its commercial impact, it carries a strong psychological pull on most Americans, which involves child worship, sentimentality and guilt. The sentimental outpouring during this period is terrific, as can be measured by the jump in suicides during it. People sometimes find too great a gap between their real world and the sentimental world demanded of them, by their surroundings.

We in the charity game take advantage of this sentimentality, just as our cousins in the for-profit world take advantage of child worship, and we both target guilt. December is the biggest giving month in the year. If we do not ask in December, we are missing an opportunity that will not come again for 12 months. We ask, and we get results. Often, we don't need to ask, so much as direct the outpouring of sentiment in a constructive manner. This time of year people literally call us asking for recommendations as to the best way they can help.

We in the charity game understand that America has a great seasonal horror of the idea of someone going hungry on Christmas or Thanksgiving Day. People bury us in stuff to make sure everyone eats on Christmas and Thanksgiving. In general, they do eat. What we need is a way to keep this food flowing all year. We know people will be hungry again the day after Christmas. We have to feed them on New Years Day, Memorial Day, Independence Day, and even on Columbus Day. But those days are not during the great season of sentimentality, and while we love the Xmas giving flood we have to depend on our core supporters, who act out of greater understanding, to keep us afloat the rest of the year.

This is not an attack on Xmas, just a statement of how it fits into our overall-begging program. Xmas is as real as April or Tuesday, and we need to use it as best we can. Xmas is fairly modern, as I said. The 19th century did not see this great buying program, and I would not be surprised if it dies of its own weight before the 21st century is over. But it is here now, and so do not be surprised to get an appeal or two in December.

All this has very little to do with Christmas. That is a religious holiday season and Christians hope it will only end with the Second Coming.

Chapter 16 Credentials

"Success and failure are both difficult to endure. Along with success come drugs, divorce, fornication, bullying, travel, meditation, medication, depression, neurosis and suicide. With failure comes failure."
Joseph Heller (novelist)

Credentials make up a large part of success in the modern business world. This is understandable because as people venture out into the world they meet more strangers than friends. If one is trying to make decisions about doing business with a stranger his credentials will help in making a prudent decision. Along with their business license, restaurants often post framed copies of good reviews. Doctors and lawyers display their diplomas and licenses, while businesses will advertise their membership in various trade or professional associations. All of these are ways to calm the customer's fears of doing business with a stranger. It is a way of saying, "someone else has already checked me out and assures you I am qualified." Third party organizations, such as the Better Business Bureau, act as clearing houses for how a business has behaved toward its customers in the past. All of this exists to allow a person to make an informed decision about starting a business relationship with a stranger.

In this regard, charities are faced with many of the same issues as regular businesses. People want to know what a charity does before committing their time and money. Charities will display their membership in area chambers of commerce, United Way chapters and other professional or civic groups. They will often publicize their mission statement, Board of Directors names and their 501(c)(3) tax exempt certificate.

The 501(c)(3) designates the part of the United States tax code that describes charities and thus differentiates them from other non-profit businesses. Other non-profit businesses exist but are not deemed charities as such. The IRS grants tax exemption to all sorts of non-profit business but each is described in a different part of the tax code and does not use the 501(c)(3) designation. Use of a 501(c)(3) means the Internal Revenue Service has looked at the setup of a business and determined that it can be exempted from paying taxes because it will be performing certain socially beneficial services. Congress has decided that certain things are so beneficial to society that a business meets its civic duty by doing these things and does not need to contribute further to the general welfare of America by paying a share of the taxes that fund the government. The IRS is in the business of collecting money so it does not close off a source of revenue without carefully checking that the agency will in fact act in such a way that benefits society as prescribed by law. If the agency's board and staff stray from the path they have outlined to the IRS without permission then they can be subject to loosing their tax exempt status as well as numerous other penalties. The IRS has a well established reputation for dealing harshly with those who break the rules.

For the potential donor, this tax status does not guarantee that the charity will do a good job of using his donation to advance its cause. It does guarantee that the United States government has looked them over very carefully and says that advancing the cause is what they are supposed to do. The prudent donor may wish to check a bit more, but the 501(c)(3) is a baseline to start from. Some charities do not have a 501(c)(3) for various reasons (the charity might be a subsidiary of another charity) but it is the first reasonable subject for a donor to ask about.

The growth of the charity industry in recent years has lead to increased scrutiny by both the government and the media. Questions about the desirability of increased regulation of the industry, reduction or elimination of tax exempt status and calls for greater government oversight have been in the news on a much more regular basis than any time before.

Long before the recent media and government interest in charities, the begging profession began to take steps at self regulation and oversight. There are several professional associations whose members are involved with some aspect of fundraising. CASE (Council for Support and Advancement of Education), NCPG (National Committee on Planned Giving) and AFP (Association of Fundraising Professionals) are examples. These organizations and others are establishing and maintaining high standards of ethics and professionalism among fundraisers.

AFP has thousands of members who, in order to join, must agree to abide by the association's ethical standards. Several years ago they developed a certification program that is meeting with widespread support in the profession. Such programs purpose is to set and maintain high professional standards.

One of the reasons I was willing to consider writing this book was a direct result of my decision to obtain my CFRE (Certified Fund Raising Executive) certificate from AFP. As I will describe, the process involved considerable writing and clarified for me exactly what my professional life had come to mean. My local AFP chapter had over 500 members and each year I encountered an increasing number of people who had taken the exam for CFRE. At first I was not concerned because one of the requirements was five years full time experience in the field of fundraising. However, as the years passed and I continued to enjoy the work I felt I had a responsibility to get certified.

The first obstacle in getting the CFRE was money. There is a hefty fee to take the exam which is only offered in certain cities at certain times of year. There was also a requirement of attendance at, a minimum of, one international fundraising conference. The conferences were held annually in a different city and they lasted several days. The cost of travel, registration, hotels and meals was several thousand dollars. My agency always encouraged the staff to continue their professional education and my boss wanted me to get the certification so I made plans. Luckily, the biggest hurdle was overcome when AFP announced that the conference would be in the city where I worked and the test would be offered at the conference. My boss agreed for the agency to pay for the test and I sent away for the registration form.

The registration form was a major shock. They wanted pages and pages of information. AFP wanted to know every detail of my fundraising over the past years. How much money had I raised and how had I raised it? How many new donors and or volunteers had I secured and from where and how? Describe the special events I had worked on. Explain in detail about any new programs I had started. Outline all my strategies for the agency and how I had implemented them. AFP wanted documentation on every class and lecture I had attended, any papers I had written, and any teaching I had done. All of my personal volunteer work in the community and for the profession had to be described in detail. The form went on and on for page after page. Each section was allotted a certain number of points for what I had done and how well I had succeeded. My score had to be high enough or I could not take the test!

This form made my past experiences, in filling out college entrance applications or employment applications seem like child's play. There was an immense amount of research into my own past I had to do. I dug out all my old appointment calendars, mileage logs, and syllabi from lectures. I also sorted through almost every manila folder I had created in the past five years to pull out data. Fortunately, I tend to keep paperwork so I knew the information was in my office or stored in the basement. Still, the process made me feel more like an archeologist than a fundraiser. At the same time the experience of documenting the history of my career helped me understand why I found begging so worthwhile. The tapestry of events, people and challenges of the years returned clearly to mind. While I knew these experiences were unique I realized that at the same time I was filling out these forms hundreds of other people across the country were also documenting their careers and that we had much in common. As I indicated, the inspiration of this book can be traced to my experiences in applying for my CFRE.

Finally, after weeks of working on the registration form it was written, copied and mailed in a cardboard box because it was too bulky for an envelope. I then settled down to wait and see if I would be allowed to take the test. A couple of months later I was duly informed by mail that I had been accepted for the exam and I began attending the exam training course AFP offered. The training course did not help my worries about the test. The test was multiple choice exam covering all aspects of fundraising from special events and mass mailing to board recruitment and planned giving. Much of the testing was based on the true life experiences of people had in the profession. A problem or circumstance would be described and three or four responses offered. We were to select the best possible response. The biggest challenge was that these were subjective, real life situations and all of the solutions offered would be good ones. We had to pick the ideal solution. When one is asked, "How much is two plus two?" there is a clear answer. When the question is how to respond to an upset donor whose name was misspelled in the annual report than the right response among three good responses is hard to discern. None of this was very reassuring when I knew that the test would be graded by a machine somewhere in New England and I would not be shown which answers I had gotten wrong but just a flat total score. There would be no opportunity to debate the testers on what was truly the best response.

I and the others taking the class were informed that people who had been in the field for a long time often did poorly because they had such a wide range of experiences they often saw nuances of advantages and disadvantages to every response and had a difficult time reaching a decision. None of this helped my confidence. I knew that a percentage of people failed the test (This turned out later to include a friend of mine who I had felt confident would pass.) and that anyone who had failed had to wait several weeks to take the test again and travel to a different city to take it.

The conference itself was great fun and very informative. On the last day the test was administered in nearby a large room. Eighty or so people took the test that day, yet I felt completely alone in that room. I had not taken a test since college more than thirty years earlier and I felt badly out of practice. I have not concentrated so hard on reading anything in years. When I finished, I had a terrible headache. A month later I received a letter informing me that my grade was a C and I had passed. I did not care if it was a D- as long as I passed.

Since then I have had to recertify once. CFRE's have to reregister every few years to get recertified but don't retake the test. They just have to prove with another pile of paperwork that they have been doing a good job somewhere in the community and helping other fundraisers do theirs. In comparison to the work for an MD, a PhD, or CPA, this is not a big deal. I also know that most of the people in fundraising do not have a CFRE and many of them are more capable than I. I am just satisfied to participate in a program that exists to tell donors that we as fundraisers want to do everything we can to justify their faith in us. As with everything in fundraising, it all comes back to the donors.

Chapter 17 Charity and Business

"Those are my principles, and if you don't like them... well, I have others."

Groucho Marx (comedian)

Depending on which survey you read, 70 to 90 percent of giving in America comes from individuals. The remaining money comes from foundations and business. It is estimated that businesses donate 10 percent or less of all the money raised for charities in the U.S. On the surface it would appear that businesses are not places to ask for charity money.

Yet charities often spend a lot of time courting business. For one, the financial numbers can be misleading. Of the money donated in America, almost a third goes to religion. This generally means the local church, temple, synagogue, mosque or other house of worship. Yet only a tiny fraction of the money business gives goes to a local house of worship. That money given to local churches almost always comes from the individuals who attend there. An attendee may give through his business, or a local church may get money from a nearby business, but on the whole businesses are not asked to support houses of worship. This is not surprising, as a house of worship is about the members, and an area business will not see a benefit unless the owner belongs to that particular house of worship. Besides, larger businesses generally have policies against giving to religions to avoid the charge of discrimination; if they give to one, they might have to give to all.

For general charities, business donations are a bit larger proportion of their possible budget. A business can often write a bigger check than an individual, especially in the name of sponsorship. Company A may benefit from the publicity of sponsoring the local school art fair, which would do Joe Jones and his wife Mary no real good. Businesses are often approached on a level of self-interest and profit that will not have the same degree of impact on an individual. "Our supporters will patronize your store because you are a friend of the beloved cause." Subsequently, most charities should and will continue to ask for business support and businessmen will have reason to be involved with charities.

However, there is a trend in the world of charity to look to the business world for more than support. Many leaders in the world of charity are turning to business for guidance and I fear that is unwise. Many in the non-profit world say we should let the for-profit model be our model and that what works for them will work for us. This trend has some strong and laudable evidence to support it, but it also has the potential of destroying philanthropy in America. Let me explain.

A business is about profit and the iron law of profit is very real. No profit, no business. No profit, no reason for the business. Something run at a loss, to amuse or in some other way to occupy the owner is a hobby not a business. I owned a business of my own for many years, and I can speak from first hand experience that profit is everything. One offers goods or services at a price higher than it costs to provide them. Any occasional short-term deviation from this model is only justified by expected long-term gain. An owner may lose to provide for better morale among their staff or to boost the business's community image, but the owner expects this to help increase profit at some point. Individuals will often give charitable donations anonymously, but that is very rare for a business. I am not saying there is anything wrong with everything being about profit; it is how business works. But it is not how charity works.

The word Charity means love. The word Philanthropy means brotherhood. Charity is about giving, not buying. Beggars can often forget this when trying to maximize the number of donors and the size of gifts. It is easy to focus on the donor's WIIFM (what's in it for me?) views and forget that he is giving, not selling. Scott Peck in "The Road Less Traveled" talks about all love involving courage or effort. Buying is for self-protection (food, clothing, shelter) or self-gratification (everything else) and you expect to get your money's worth. Philanthropy is your love for your brother, even if he is a stranger on the other side of the planet, or a dog at the pound. The charity exists as a conduit to let one's love flow to one's brother. It has no other reason to exist. If it blocks that flow of love, misdirects it, impedes it, or in any other way stifles it the charity will stop being about charity. If a charity takes on the iron law of profit as its law, it is no longer a charity. It may meet the legal, but not the human requirements. Let me give you an example of an institution that seems to have aspects of a charity but is not.

In America today there is a large organization. It has many hardworking people, and it gathers a vast amount of money that is often used to help all sorts of people, with all sorts of problems. It is the Internal Revenue Service. Nobody thinks it is a charity. In many countries their version of the IRS is the only game in town. In such countries work in the community to better the lives of the citizens comes from government, tax funded, programs. However, in America, we still value the direct decision of an individual to help his brother as he sees fit. This is philanthropy in America. It works for a lot of reasons but the most important is the direct flow of love, from sister to sister, brother to brother.

The IRS is an example of a government agency. It works very well (try to dodge your taxes and you may find out just how well). Business philosophy works well for business. For business profit is the most important consideration. But charity is neither one of these things and adopting either as the new model for charity will, as in Aesop's fable, kill the goose that lays the eggs of purest gold.

Chapter 18 Public Relations

"Trying to determine what is going on in the world by reading newspapers is like trying to tell the time by watching the second hand of a clock."
Ben Hecht (Hollywood screenwriter)

Public relations can be a large part of the begging game. The perception of the charity by the public, whether by donors or non donors, will play a big role in attracting new donors and maintaining old ones.

Public relations experts use a language all their own. Press releases, branding, marketing, PR, advertising and media relations are frequently used words. As this is not a training manual I will try to avoid them. Also these words may change meaning and go in and out of favor.

In reality, most professionals in the non-profit world think of one thing when they think of public relations, reporters who can give them free publicity. Obviously, beggars love anything free. A charity might be noticed more with a full-page advertisement in a local newspaper, than in a short one-column story. The beggar should bear in mind that the one column story is free and the advertisement costs money. Also, Americans see so many ads, that they mostly ignore them. People reading a newspaper will read the stories and skip the ads. People watching TV will leave the room during the ads. This simple fact drives professionals in advertising crazy.

Reporters can be the gateway to the public's attention. If the public hears the charity's story and cares about it, they will help. And reporters usually like helping charities tell their story. A local business introducing a new product is less likely to get a front-page story, even on a slow news day, than a local charity helping sick children with a new treatment. What the press refers to as human-interest stories are more often about people helping people than people selling to people.

At the same time reporters will not hesitate to expose and condemn any charity seen as doing wrong. A charity doing wrong is news and reporters are all about news. The possibility of an unfavorable news story is the part of public relations that everyone in the profession dreads, but had better be ready for. This is the area of crisis management.

Crisis Management is a term that makes the adrenaline flow for anyone dealing with reporters. Suddenly, words like mistake, human error, misfortune or regrettable incident become negligence, irresponsibility, mismanagement or disgrace. And if the reporters are yelling loud enough the charity's management is faced with the possibility of other words being used. The real danger comes from words like willful neglect, liability, lawsuit or crime.

I know a man who had run a children's summer camp for many years. One summer there was an incident with one of the campers and the campers parents claimed their child had been assaulted. They filed suit and contacted the local press with the story. One of the stations carried the story on the evening news. There were follow up stories in the media, some of which made the camp look very bad. The camp director had a terrible dilemma because his attorneys insisted he say very little to the press until the suit went to court. After many months, the camp was vindicated in court and it was shown that what had actually happened was clearly not as serious as had been portrayed. A while after this was all over I asked the camp director to be part of a panel of reporters and charity public relations people to address the issue of crisis management. The man had retired and was available. When he related the story it was clear he was still very angry about how some members of the press had treated him and his camp. He explained that as part of his public relations response he had contacted as many of the camp's supporters as possible and explained that he could not make public statements but that he hoped they would remember the fine reputation the camp had and his many years of service and hold judgment until all the facts were in. His donors stayed loyal and the storm passed but it was a tremendous emotional strain on everyone connected with the camp. News stories hit in just a few minutes but the American judicial system moves much more slowly and the camp supporters had to wait a long time for vindication.

A non-profit can be destroyed. A charity can be sued for an amount that financially wrecks it. Even a lawsuit a charity wins can wreck it. If a charity receives enough bad publicity that its donors stop giving, it can go bankrupt. The fact that it is vindicated in a courtroom several years later does not bring it back to life. My friend, the camp director had to move swiftly and effectively to retain his donors and avoid that fate.

In the end, a charity has a clearer moral duty in its public relations policy than a business. Even if a story must be told through the filter of a reporter, it must be honestly told. The phrases "cover up" or "stone wall" cannot be part of a charity's media plan. Charities ride the wave of the public's love and trust and they have to expect a greater sense of anger and betrayal from the public if they fail in that trust.

In 1992, there was a scandal, involving misuse of funds, with the national office of United Way and the head of the United Way went to jail. That was a long time ago and there have been many business scandals in America since but that one has been neither forgotten nor forgiven. I have given many talks for the local United Way over the years and I still get questions and concerns about that incident even though it was long ago and in a different part of the country. When it comes to a betrayal of trust the public has a long memory.

The public can demonstrate it has a long memory about something negative even without a reporter being involved. We routinely have volunteer groups come help at the agency. Once we had a group of men volunteer from a large suburban church. While they were inside working someone broke into the car of one of the volunteers. The volunteer came out to the parking lot and found his side window smashed and a few items on the seat stolen. We profusely apologized but he was not too upset and said his insurance would cover it.

The next time I visited that church, two or three people mentioned the car break in. I was not pleased about that because it gave the impression that coming to help us put one's car at risk. Still, I assumed it was nothing important and I had heard the last of it. Over the years I have made dozens of presentations about my agency at that church. In almost every case, when I am done speaking and am standing around visiting with the congregation someone will mention that my agency is where one of the church members had his car broken into. It is helpful to remember that these people are friends of the agency who support its programs generously. Unfortunately, the image of the agency as a place of risk if one goes there to help has become imbedded in that church. Word of mouth has moved that one incident of bad publicity through the congregation more effectively than TV and radio combined.

It is useful to remember Jesus' words in the Bible, "Behold, I send you forth as sheep in the midst of wolves: be ye therefore wise as serpents, and harmless as doves." (Matthew 10:16.) A charity has a duty to be honest with reporters without catering to the reporter's need for controversy or haste. A common honest answer in many crises is, "I don't know but I will find out and tell you as soon as I am able." This is often the case, because any problem is generally accompanied by a lot of confusion as to what really happened. But reporters don't like that answer because they need a story at once. However," I don't know" is often the best and most honest answer. After all, we want to be honest. It is not our job to create news.

In the same vein, we should never speculate. Reporters love to ask "what if" questions to get controversy. In a twenty minute interview, a ten second answer to a "what if" question may be the only thing on the evening news. The honest answer is "It is not appropriate for me to engage in speculation."

On the whole, I have had an excellent relationship with reporters, and have seen them help numerous charities. They have given us wonderful coverage on events and several television newscasters routinely act as master of ceremonies at our fundraisers. As I mentioned in the story about the camp director, several reporters volunteered to sit on the discussion panel to help the audience understand what they were doing when they covered a story. Remember, a reporter covering a story is not there as a volunteer for the charity. For that matter, neither is a politician or a citizen off the street. That does not make them enemies; it just means they may have a different agenda than supporting the charity. A reporter is always looking for a good story just as a politician is always looking for a good campaign issue but that may not be helpful for the charity. Finally, no matter what you hear, good or bad, remember the old adage, "Don't believe everything you read in the newspapers."

Chapter 19 Serenity

"By three methods we may learn wisdom: First, by reflection, which is noblest; second, by imitation, which is easiest; and third by experience, which is the bitterest."
Confucius (Chinese philosopher)

As I have mentioned, one of the problems in persuading people to donate their money is that they fear not having enough for themselves. This fear may be reflected in a lot of different ways and affects how we ask some people for money. It also explains why one charity is better received by the donor.

If a person wants to buy status in the community, he may be willing to give to a cause popular among the rich and important. The big gala event, with lots of rich famous people around, may be what is needed to get him to write a check.

If people's professional reputation is based to some degree on where they went to school then they may be more open to an appeal from their alumni association then from the Red Cross. Doctors, lawyers, architects or MBAs may feel the need to support the good name of their Alma Matter more than someone who dropped out their sophomore year and went on to become a successful stand up comic, rock star or billionaire entrepreneur.

In these cases, the donor is both helping the charity and buying something for themselves. Their picture in the society page or their college being noted as a top school for people in their field is, in itself, a reward. It can give them the same satisfaction as a new Rolls Royce or an office in the big new building downtown. They are willing to pay for prestige. If a beggar is working for a charity that does not offer the prestige desired by that type of donor, then the beggar is wasting time attempting to get a gift.

Another donor might leave money to the charity in their will but not while they are alive. If a charity needs money now, such people will be of no help. It is interesting to note that these people are often driven by a fear of running out of money, a fear which sometimes appears to have little reasonable basis. One lady, I know of, refused to a pledge to her church because she claimed that she might be tying up money she would need for herself. The woman was in her eighties and had well over twenty million dollars. This is an example of poverty existing only between the ears. You will sometimes hear older people talk of the problems of living on a fixed income, which can be difficult. But every once in a while it becomes hard to sympathize or even understand, if you discover the income is fixed at six or even seven figures per year. We all can suffer from this problem to a degree. Most people view growing old as a time when the body becomes weaker and less dependable. This can cause a fear of loss of independence and the need of more help from others. While it is true we live longer and healthier than ever before, the awareness that we might outlive the money saved up during the working years is a real fear. The image of being poor when we are too old and sick, to work can terrify some of us beyond rational thought.

On the other hand, there are many wonderful people who have tithed all their lives and continue to do so after retirement. They may not be wealthy and their last illness may take everything, but they are not worried about such issues. They live by the words of Jesus as recorded in Mathew 6:27, "Can any of you by worrying add a single hour to your span of life?" People who allow this truth to govern their lives are serene. The word serenity plays a major role in long term charitable commitment. I don't think we, as Americans, fully understand its value or its nature.

Serenity is neither fatalism nor folly. It is not necessarily optimism but it is most certainly not cynicism. It flows out of patience, prudence and charity. It requires both courage and wisdom. You can never be part of the herd and be serene. Money clearly does not buy it, because history has shown us many serene individuals who were poor. Faith in something greater than oneself is a definite prerequisite (whether religion, country, a cause or a life philosophy does not seem to matter). It is freedom in the world and from the world. It is a pearl of great price.

Serenity is rare, because the world does not encourage it. Serene people don't make good consumers, because so much of modern marketing is based on fear, dissatisfaction, envy or pride. People who do not understand will mislabel serenity as laziness, stupidity, callousness, or even treason, none of which are valid. Serene people will support a charity because they believe in what it does, but they will understand if the charity fails. We once had a donor underwrite a project that turned out to be a complete failure. A board member called him up to apologize for the failure and he said, "When that money was in my bank account it did not make me infallible so there is no reason for me to think when I gave it to you people it would make you infallible." He has continued to donate to this day.

Serenity means letting go of what we cannot hold anyway. We cannot control the future, change the past or bend the world to our will. A serene person understands what he cannot control and does not waste energy or time trying. Serene people laugh and cry, but they are not sentimental or bitter. If such people make us irritable, it is our own envy at work. Relax, they won't bite.

Chapter 20 The Danger of Words

"I like your Christ; I do not like your Christians.

Your Christians are so unlike your Christ."

Gandhi (political and spiritual leader of India)

I was recently told a volunteer left a committee he was on for a number of years. A breakdown in communication between us caused him to feel I had dropped him from the committee. In years past I had sometimes contacted members of the committee to see if they wished to remain on but I had not yet done so this year and he decided he was fired.

At first I was angry and hurt that someone was accusing me of something unfairly. Later, I came to realize this is an example of the danger of words. The chairperson reporting what had happened seemed as dumbfounded as I was so I do not think there was any intent to mislead me about what had occurred. I did not get to speak to the person first hand, so I can know nothing of the tone of the remarks, or how the conversation flowed. While I did not get to speak directly to the volunteer he clearly had a complaint.

In working with volunteers and donors, the development staff walks through a minefield. A failure to compliment is often as disastrous as a deliberate slur. All sorts of people want to help your cause. Some are easy going and some are intense. Some like to laugh while others are serious. One must never forget the staff-volunteer relationship is a working relationship, not a friendship. Unlike in the business arena, your volunteers and donors are not held in place by the common need for financial income. Workers can be held on jobs that they hate, with coworkers and bosses that they despise, by the need for a paycheck. The volunteer is a free agent with no financial pressure to make him help you. Upset him, and he can drop you like a hot rock, with no personal downside for him.

It is vital that the staff and board of any charity listen to the volunteers and donors. While one must never let these people move the charity away from the core values and purpose of the organization, they are entitled to give input. They also deserve to be appreciated. This is where listening is vital. Different people help for different reasons and will want different types of responses from the charity.

Over the years, I have had volunteers offended that we gave them a small "thank you" gift. They never want to see the agency's resources wasted on such things. Alternatively, I have had donors dissatisfied if they feel the charity does not show tangible appreciation for their efforts. Some volunteers expect to have input into the running of the organization, while others look for the escape from responsibility by doing simple tasks. The real trick comes because people do not always reveal their real needs and wants, and sometimes don't even know them.

I once worked for a charity where a lady volunteered on a regular basis for a number of years and repeatedly stated she did not need any thanks and to not bother with recognition gifts. We honored her wishes and did not push our gratitude on her. One day my boss was at a meeting attended by this lady's pastor. My boss thanked him for the great work the volunteer was doing. The pastor was amazed to discover both the extent long history of her work. Not long after the pastor used the story of the lady and her years of dedication in a sermon about taking the message of God into the world. The lady was both stunned and thrilled. She told me she would never forget it and how that statement of praise and support coming from her own church made everything she had done worthwhile. It has been many years since I have talked to her but I have been informed she is as busy as ever. I was struck by the fact that while she shunned thanks unexpected praise from a different source validated everything she had done.

Over the years, I have been chewed out by donors, volunteers, and board members for doing both too much and too little to thank people. I have not enjoyed the chewing, but I do not expect to die from criticism. The major concern, which I share with all other professionals, is the danger of the angry donor who goes around telling everyone how bad we are. This is an amazing phenomenon when you think about it. Here is someone who has given time and money to a cause. At some point, they get unhappy with how they have been treated and leave. This departure is rarely about the basic work the charity does. Instead, it is usually some personal conflict they have with a staff person, a board member, or another volunteer. They may spend years blasting the charity without realizing they are not hurting the person they are angry with, but the charity itself. Word of mouth is still recognized in advertising as the most powerful advertising of all. Just as you will not try a restaurant where your friend said he got food poisoning, you will not support a charity your friend claims is badly run. Yet if one confronts the person doing the complaining and asks if he wants the disease to remain uncured, or the children to go hungry, the complaining person will be deeply hurt. He still cares about the cause and never thinks about his words as doing harm to that cause.

Years ago there was a town in the part of the country where I lived that was trying to get a large national company to locate a new production plant there. One person supporting the project was the school principal. He knew that a new business meant tax money for the school plus more jobs for his students. A company team visited the town to gather data as to the advisability of building there. They interviewed a number of people including the principal. The night before there had been a break-in with some minor vandalism at the school and the principal had been up most of the night with the police and cleaning staff getting the school ready for classes. As a result the principal was late getting to the meeting and when someone made a joke about it he lost his temper. He complained about the police department and the difficulty in getting professional help in the town to repair the broken glass and locks. The meeting then went on and everyone expressed the hope that the new plant would be coming soon. The production plant was never built. The team's report included the principal's comments about the police and the lack of repair facilities and the company picked another town that did not appear to have these problems. A few words spoken in frustration by someone who loved the town and wanted it to grow were enough to block its growth for years. This example could just as easily happen to a charity seeking a grant. In fundraising we have to be vigilant about what we say and when we say it. Words have power and as with all power, they can do harm.

Chapter 21 A History Lesson

"History teaches us that men and nations behave wisely once they have exhausted all other alternatives."
Abba Eban (Israeli diplomat and politician)

"Why do we even need charities? Why can't we help those in need and skip the middleman? I want my money to help needy people not pay the salaries of administrators and fund raisers."

These statements are common in America today. People want a guarantee that their gift will help solve a problem not perpetuate an unnecessary institution. The concern is a real one but needs to be more deeply considered. A spokesman for a major foundation told of how he responded to such a complaint from a prospective donor. He told the donor to convert his planned donation into cash and stand on the street passing out the money. By doing so, none of the money would be wasted on administration, public relations, fundraising or any of the other aspects of a charity that were not direct support to the needy.

As the foundation speaker explained, the problem with passing out ten-dollar bills on a street corner is you are no closer to solving a problem or meeting a need. You have no way of sorting out if the needy are getting the money, or if ten dollars will solve their problems. It took the clear image of the meaningless act of passing out ten dollar bills to people on the street to show the donor he had neither the time nor the knowledge to direct his gift where it would help. In fact, he needed the services of an institution that would get the lion's share of his gift to those in need with only a small overhead to keep the institution in place so it could perform the same service for the next needy donor.

A short history lesson helps bring the value of charitable institutions into prospective. In ancient times, communities were small and the direct contact between the needy and those with resources was easy. The great anthropologist Margaret Meade stated that the earliest sign of civilization was a healed femur; to find among the bones of an early human a tended and healed fracture in the upper leg. Such a broken bone would make it impossible for the person to hunt or gather food for themselves for several weeks. That meant someone else had been willing to fend for this individual for a long period of time, with no assurance the injured party would ever walk again. Meade said no healed femurs are found in cultures where the survival of the fittest reign, or where the weakest necessarily fall by the wayside. A healed femur meant someone cared. The Bible describes the duty of farmers to leave some of the harvest for the local widows and orphans to gather. In many early societies friends and neighbors would routinely help build the house or barn of a neighbor. In many cultures, when a man advanced in wealth or property he would hold a party for the community in celebration and everyone would receive food and gifts from the host.

During the feudal age the lord of the manor was expected to take care of the basic needs of the peasants. They gave him a share of their crops and helped maintain his castle while he provided protection, settled disputes and provided for those in need. A lord who did not feed the local widows and orphans the excess from his own table was viewed as wicked by everyone. Beggars could expect alms from those better off than themselves. On great religious holidays even the poorest in the community could expect food and warmth at the manor house.

During the later Middle Ages as the population in Europe grew it also became more mobile. Wars and plagues upset the traditional feudal land relationships and people moved about looking for work and food. The old, stable, rural ways of people in the community caring for the less fortunate was breaking down. Groups of beggars went from manor house to manor house seeking help. In some cases these groups might shift from beggars to extortionists or robbers as the need and opportunity arose. The old English nursery rhyme, "Hark, hark, the dogs do bark. The beggars are coming to town. Some in rags and some in tags and some in velvet gowns" describes these beggar bands. More people were moving to the cities for work and this new urban population added to the growing sense of alienation between the people and their traditional lords.

During the middle ages in Europe many of the institutions we are so familiar with sprang up. Hospitals were some of the earliest institutions established to help the needy. Wealth could be directed to such an institution where people could receive the best care available at the time. Insane asylums, orphanages, and other buildings specifically designed to meet a certain need on a permanent basis began to appear. Religious orders to help the poor, sick, and lost began the work that would someday be social workers, nurses, medics, and even fire and rescue workers. An example were the Hospitaler Knights of the Crusades who set up places for pilgrims on their way to Jerusalem might find food, shelter and salves for the sunburn so common in the desert. Such places of hospitality and care eventually became, as the name implies, the modern hospital. The monks of the abbey of St. Bernard, who rescued travelers lost in the snow-covered winter passes with the help of the famous St. Bernard dogs, were the fore runners of modern search and rescue teams. Modern day social workers and medics can see their ancestors in the membership of the order of St. Francis of Assisi.

This process of institutions and organizations taking over the charitable efforts of individual neighbors did not occur overnight nor in the neat order described in history books. The change came because people wanted to help but realized they did not have the time or the expertise to get the appropriate help to the person in need at the appropriate time. With the increasing mobility of society particularly in the Industrial Revolution, people were not as familiar with their neighbors as they were during the more static earlier periods in Europe. Some of the institutions, which resulted, are over a thousand years old and some are brand new. Still, their existence has not ended the older system of neighbor helping neighbor. When you take a sack of the surplus tomatoes that you grew in your garden to the elderly couple next door you are involved in a community activity as old as recorded history and as Margaret Meade noted, even older than written history.

My point is that these institutions serve a purpose other than self-perpetuation and they have proved their worth over time. The needy person often finds that an established institution, even with all its bureaucracy, can be a bigger help than the most caring individual amateur philanthropist. Let me give you a small bit of modern history.

At a homeless shelter there is a very nice couple I will call 'Smith' who just had a baby. They are from a foreign country where crime and corruption are rampant. The demand for bribes from local gangs to allow them keep their business open was making it impossible for the Smiths to make ends meet. Mrs. Smith, through her job, met a tourist couple from America, who took an interest in her and her husband. The Americans said that if the Smiths wanted to come to America they, the Americans, would be happy to sponsor their admission and get them jobs. The Smiths felt this was a dream come true but they knew they could not get a work visa. The American couple said not to worry about that and just get a tourist visa. So the Smiths saved, worked and sold what little they had and finally got enough money set aside and came to America on a tourist visa.

When they got here they went to see their American friends. The American man informed them that he and his wife were getting a divorce, thus his life was very messed up at the moment and he was no longer interested in sponsoring them. The Smiths were then in real trouble. They could go home but in getting out they had angered the gangsters. For them to return home would be to face possible beatings or murder from the gangsters. At the least, they would be jobless and homeless.

The Smiths then got into worse trouble here in America. A group of people promised to help them stay here. These people informed the Smiths that the process was long and expensive and a number of payments for each step would be needed. Their new "friends" took all their money and then refused to help the Smiths. It was at this point that they came to the shelter.

They have been at the shelter for some time because neither of them could get work. They had overstayed their tourist visas and the government would not issue a work visa. By overstaying their tourist visa they are in violation of the law, and the government is very strict about not giving visas to people once they have broken the rules. This is the result of the waves of legal and illegal immigration America is dealing with as well as the increased security since 9/11.

Customs and Immigration could not ignore the law or their own rules. The Smiths would have to return to their own country and there try to be readmitted into the United States. While that is the law and it exists for our well being, the result would be that they would not be readmitted and that they will be both broke and in danger. When last I saw them their final appeal had been rejected and they were going to be deported in a few days. No one at the shelter wanted to have to tell these people about the rejection letter. Everyone liked them and wanted things to work out for them. Both worked hard at the shelter and were happy to take on any task.

As I am writing this a ray of hope has begun to shine. The staff and board of the shelter brought this case to the local congressman. His staff is looking into the matter and the couple's deportation has been put on hold.

This story illustrates the need for professional institutions. The American tourist couple meant well. They wanted to help some poor deserving people in a direct way. They were caring and determined to help. However, a human life is a big responsibility. Ask any parent. When you take responsibility for someone, that responsibility does not stop because you no longer have the time, resources or energy to deal with it. American's love their "can do" spirit but it had better be real spirit and not vanity. If you cut someone's lifeline it does not matter if you act from desperation or mere indifference. If you cut it they fall just as far either way. An institution generally has multiple lifelines and can do more to avoid letting someone fall.

A needy person is best directed to professionals for help. It may not be as personal but one must know their own capacity for hard work, suffering and disappointment before taking on someone else's life. As I said the American couple meant well but they put this nice family at risk and their only hope was the homeless shelter and its staff and board. Fortunately, that dry old institution may have the resources and dedication to squeeze a happy ending out of this nightmare. Only time will tell.

(Post script: Months after these events, I was informed the family had been granted the right to stay and both are now working and raising their child.)

Chapter 22 Sweat Equity

"The desire for virtue is frustrated in many men of good will by the distaste they instinctively feel for the false virtues of those who are supposed to be holy. Sinners have a very keen eye for false virtues and a very exacting idea of what virtue should be in a good man. If in the men who are supposed to be good they only see a "virtue" which is effectively less vital then their own vices they will conclude that virtue has no meaning, and will cling to what they have although they hate it."

Thoughts in Solitude

Thomas Merton (Trappist monk and author)

Over the years I have observed more interest in volunteering particularly by young people. On the national level there has been a large push to get people interested in volunteer service, starting with George H. Bush and the Thousand Points of Light Program. This was the biggest government effort to get people involved is volunteering to help others since the Peace Corp and Vista programs of the 1960's.

On the local level, volunteering is now a graduation requirement for students in many high schools. Over the last few years I have received many phone calls from students and parents inquiring about volunteer opportunities. While my agency normally uses hundreds of volunteers in a year we do not have an unlimited capacity and it can be a challenge to match our needs with a high school student's schedule and experience. Still, we always try because we want and need volunteers!

We have also experienced increasing traffic in volunteer youth groups. These groups can come from all over the nation and be all sizes. The most common are church youth groups of one to three dozen from local area churches or synagogues. While our agency is a mission project of a main line protestant denomination we have always been happy to get help from anyone. From a time long before I came on board there had been a strong tie to the area Jewish Community Center and each summer we had a number of their older youth volunteer as councilors with our summer camp. Other church denominations in the area also look for places their youth can help.

One of the most interesting changes in youth volunteers has been the number of contacts from around the country by organizations that coordinate youth "mission trips" for various denominations. These coordinating organizations are looking to place a group for a day or a week in a charity they can help that is away from home. It is not unusual for a youth group to spend much of the year raising money at home to finance a trip to a distant location were they can help out for a few days. Because of school requirements and family vacation plans I see two thirds of these groups in June and July. Unfortunately, my agency cannot accommodate all the requests. Over the years I have developed a close relationship with a number of area agencies and can often suggest alternate volunteer sites to the groups I turn down.

The main reason I turn people away is a common problem with many charities that use volunteers. The problem is the often, mentioned, issue of limited resources. There are just not enough people available to properly train, coordinate and supervise the youth groups that want to help. Where I worked volunteers were part of the development program and this is fairly common in small to medium sized charities. Volunteer time like donations of goods or money is something a charity asks for and thanks people for and it is normal to put all these things in the agency beggar's lap.

Whenever I accepted a youth group, the actual work they did was generally determined by the man responsible for building maintenance. He has worked with youth groups for years and never failed to make sure they are properly supervised and encouraged. However, the maintenance of the building was his first responsibility. In June and July we generally had about eighty to a hundred and thirty inner city youth in our day camp in the building. This was in addition to the ninety plus children in the day care, the adults in the food pantry and thrift shop and anyone else who walked in off the street looking for help. In other words, the building was very busy and very noisy and the maintenance staff has a lot of work to do. For the head of maintenance to take time out to train and supervise a group of ten to twenty youth was a strain.

Generally speaking, the younger a group of volunteers is the less they can do and the more supervision they need. Adult groups are the most capable and if one or two of them have carpentry, plumbing or electrical experience they are worth their weight in gold. There are always repairs for such knowledgeable people. We would allow adults and college students to paint because while they were not as good as professionals they could be taught the basics of painting quickly and would generally have the maturity to stay with a job until completed. High schools students were a bit more doubtful as painters. They might tire before the job was completed or get restless and start playing with the paint. Almost every high school painting crew had at least one student run a loaded paint roller down someone else's back. Over the years we learned it was better to let the high school groups concentrate on outside paint jobs where dripping paint fell on the grass rather than on an inside carpet.

There were a number of other tasks we needed on our building due to the constant wear and tear of several thousand clients including hundreds of active children. The staff always wanted the building to be a clean, attractive and pleasant place for those who came to us for help. The work of various volunteer groups made that and some other aspects of the program possible. We were happy to have them but it was a strain on our staff to keep them directed and motivated in such a way that their work helped us and that the volunteers understood how it helped. I have learned over the years that if people understand how their work fits into the overall operation of the charity they feel much happier and are more productive even if the particular task they are doing is not very interesting. I also know how important it is to thank them for their efforts. Over the years we have worked some volunteers very hard and the only reward I could offer was our heartfelt thanks.

When a volunteer group would arrive I would normally give them a tour of the building, tell them about the various programs and explain the importance of their work. I would then take then to the maintenance director and he would explain the project in detail, help the group leaders assign tasks and distribute the needed supplies and tools. Once the youth started work, the maintenance director would routinely check their progress and be on call to answer questions and find additional needed tools. Along with this he was doing his regular job and responding to the frequent requests and problems that are part of the maintenance of a large busy building. As I have said, in June and July he was under a great deal of pressure. He worked very well with the youth and their leaders and groups often requested the chance to come back and work for him again. He was sincerely dedicated to ensuring that the volunteers had the chance to be useful and productive. Still, during the summer if I came down to his desk and announced that a work group had canceled, he generally received the news with the relief of a man reprieved from execution. More often than I wish to remember I had to tell him that I had agreed to host a group larger than he could reasonably supervise or worse, had scheduled two groups on the same day. As a result, my approach was greeted with the dry wit and sarcasm that was his only response to whatever mess I was dumping on his head. Such remarks as, "Oh lucky me; here comes, his Excellency, Mr. Lewis to bring some sunshine into my day" were common. I have always felt the remarks at my expense were perfectly reasonable because the work load I was often giving him might have justified his sinking a pickaxe into my head. Yet, when the mob of volunteers arrived he would plunge right in and provide them with a meaningful and productive day of work. He is a very great man and a credit to the agency.

We are happy to get volunteers and donors from outside the church denomination that sponsors the agency. In talking to other church based charities I know that this is very common. Clergy of various denominations have told me they are just as likely to get people involved in the church because a friend invites them to help at the church's charity than because someone invites them to attend services on Sunday. The agency has become a mutually beneficial way to connect to another church.

Several years ago, a youth leader of a large church in the area called me. He was looking for some "hands on" experience his youth could get in helping others. I asked him to come out and look at our program to see if it might meet his needs.

He was very impressed with the program and wanted his church to become involved. I gave him a variety of ways his membership could help both as one time projects and as ongoing activities. Subsequently his youth have helped landscape our property and put on a concert for our day care. Other members of the church have become involved on an individual basis.

For some of the established charities affiliated with church denominations that are not growing or are in decline the building of a relationship with non denominational churches or churches of other denominations may be appropriate. For a new church in an area or a church that does not have a local mission project building a relationship with the ongoing mission project of another church gives the congregation an immediate opportunity to experience "hands on" service. It avoids the delay and expense of setting up a mission program.

There was a study done not long ago by a large denomination. It found that people are more likely to join a church that has an active outreach mission program of some type. The people who join may not become involved in the program but they will feel much better about joining a congregation that is actively helping others outside the church. This attitude apparently runs across all ages and political ideologies.

For the established charity it provides a new group of enthusiastic supporters and a new revenue source. For both groups it minimizes any issues of doctrine or denominational control. Both groups are there to help needy people and not to talk church politics. Staffs of many established charities are not necessarily members of the denomination which sponsors the charity. Thus, newcomers from another church are less likely to feel like outsiders. Even if there is a sense on the part of the church that started the charity that they are losing ownership of their mission, they might be more willing to surrender control if they feel sure the mission will go on.

Over the years the major cities of America have witnessed an interesting phenomenon. In the inner city you see churches with one name on the sign out front but another name carved on the building cornerstone. As the populations of neighborhoods have changed, the local church building has often been abandoned. Some have been demolished, some converted to other uses but many have simply changed congregation and denomination. The simple reality is that a church building is not a particularly great design for anything but a church. At the same time, if you are growing a new congregation, no style of building better suits your needs than a church.

What is true for old church buildings is also true for church mission projects. If for whatever reason the people who started and built up the mission are no longer able to maintain it at its current level that does not mean the mission is not still needed. For a growing congregation there is nothing better for its health and prosperity than helping people outside the church. Why would a church not step into some ongoing work that needs their involvement at once? Why wait three, five or seven years to reach the goal of the long range planning committee when you can feed the hungry, visit prisoners, or shelter the homeless starting now?

For the people who built up the program and watched it grow and prosper over the years, the issue is the same as the fate of the old church when the congregation moves to a new location. Is it not much better to see the building you loved used by people to worship the God you love even if they do it in a way you do not? It is much better seeing another congregation in your church than to see it as a warehouse, bowling alley or abandoned wreck. Would church members also feel it better that the mission their church began continued, even if by others than have it stop? Most will want the mission to continue no matter who runs it.

This passing the torch will not be the best solution for every mission project in need of additional support. But anyone concerned about the future of a particular mission project might want to consider it.

Chapter 23 The Board

"We succeed in enterprises which demand the positive qualities we possess, but we excel in those which can also make use of our defects."
Alexis de Tocqueville (French political thinker and historian)

Most charities have a Board of Directors. About the only exceptions are charities that are some sort of subset or division of a larger business entity. To receive tax exempt status from the IRS, an independent organization must have a Board of Directors. It is almost impossible to get around this rule and still gain tax exempt status. A few years ago, the IRS announced it had issued its one millionth 501(c)(3) or tax exempt business license to operate. Since over a million organizations now have this tax exempt status it is reasonable to assume there are a lot of board members in the United States.

I have worked with Boards and sat on Boards. They are at the center of all fund raising. A development department which is not closely involved with the Board will not have an easy time raising money. The simple fact that is that people give to causes they have some sense of commitment to or involvement with. There is no group of people more involved with an organization or more responsible for its basic direction than the Board. The Board of Directors directs the charity. Who can have a more legitimate sense of involvement or ownership of a charity than the members of the Board?

Yet, it is not uncommon to find Board members who look upon their charity as an alien entity. They may have a vague understanding that they have agreed to lend their name to something but they have no sense of ownership and in many cases cannot even tell what the charity does. They do not attend the Board meetings or any other functions the charity has and contribute nothing of their time, talent or resources to the charity's welfare. They may be listed on the charity's letterhead but none of the staff, clients or other Board members could hope to pick them out of a police lineup if asked. How can this be?

The answer in part has to do with the sheer volume of Board members. With over a million charities there are a lot of Board members and they can't all be famous. The Metropolitan Opera Company in New York is very famous and popular. Membership on that Board is sought after by many wealthy and important people. They have a long waiting list and a new Board member must make a large donation to be accepted. Unfortunately, local charities do not have the prestige of the Met to offer potential Board members. The charity's leaders can set whatever standards of participation and support they want but that does not mean they will have to beat off all the rush of potential Board members. They may find that they are going, hat in hand, to all sorts of people just to fill out their Board's vacancies, much less having a waiting list.

After all, Board membership is work, and most people feel they have plenty of work to do without volunteering for more. This fact can lead charity leaders into making an unfortunate but very human error. The recruiters for the Board may often minimize the amount of work and responsibility needed to be a Board member. One group where this can be a particular problem is with celebrities.

Celebrities are often highly prized as Board members for several reasons. A celebrity's name may help get publicity for the charity. People may want to become involved with a charity in hopes of getting to know the celebrity. Also, people often view a celebrity as a meaningful endorsement of a charity. These factors will often cause charities to promise the celebrity that they do not need to do anything but list their name on the board.

The problem is that this situation leads to resentment from the other Board members. Positions on a board taken by "in name only" members means that more work must be shared by the rest of the Board. Hard working Board members will have a legitimate complaint if they discover they are second class members, who do the work, but are seen as being of less importance to the charity. They will really be upset when they discover the celebrity's name is supposed to help bring in money but they are the ones who are going to have to go out and do the asking.

Yes, that is correct. Board members must ask for money. And they must donate money themselves. Those two facts are another reason it is not all that easy to recruit and keep good Board members. Times have changed for Boards. Twenty or thirty years ago members were much less likely to be required to help raise money or to donate money themselves. That is no longer true. Many foundations in America today will not even consider making a grant to a charity that cannot show 100% of its Board donates to the charity. Time, talent and treasure are all required of today's Board member, and recruiters for a charity will be very foolish not to make this clear at the very beginning of recruitment.

The need for Board members to ask for donations goes back to the issue of involvement and ownership. Who can speak more clearly and completely as to a charity's needs than the people directing it? Who understands its place in the community better? Finally who has a more legitimate right to ask for help than those people who have volunteered to lead the charity in its good work? There is no more compelling moment in fund raising than when a potential donor is meeting with a member of the Board and the Board member says, "I have explained our needs to you. I have already committed myself to this cause with all the resources at my disposal. Will you now step forward and partner with me in this great work? I will always be personally grateful to you." Words of that sort, spoken from one charitable person to another are very hard to ignore. Very few professional beggars can make a more effective appeal.

Thus, Board members must ask for money and they must donate money. They must formulate policy, render decisions on operational issues, keep themselves knowledgeable about the charity and its future, attend meetings and events, and try to interest others in their cause. In addition, they must do all of this for free. Unlike regular businesses, charities do not generally compensate their Boards. All this would make you think anyone who volunteers to sit on a Board must be a bit unhinged. After all, these people cannot even be starry eyed idealists living an illusion as to how great their charity is. These people are on the Board! They know exactly how the place is run because they are running it. They are under no illusions about the place that they direct. Otto von Bismarck once said, "Laws are like sausages, it is better not to see them being made." Board members cannot avoid seeing their rules and directions being made because they are making them.

Yet each year, millions of these people keep the charities of America running. That fact speaks volumes about their dedication, perseverance and strong character.

There are few things an American can do that are more worthwhile than serving a term on the Board of a local charity. There is always some small local program that will be happy to have help. It may not feel great the whole time they are doing it because, as Bismarck noted, sausage making can be rather gross. On the other hand, a person may find that like many Board members he or she will be willing to serve again once the term is up. We have one lady who served in several positions on the board including the finance committee. She also got her husband to be on the board and he was part of the group that set up the development department and hired me. (That decision alone marks him as a great man in my eyes.) Over the years they have been involved with the agency in good times and difficult ones. They have helped with large projects and small and have donated and asked others to donate. As a result of their years of selfless dedication and leadership they were both voted lifetime members of the board. They both love the agency and never tire of helping it. I can personally testify to the fact that the agency's present strength and size is in large part due to their years of work.

If someone goes onto a Board with their eyes wide open and their sleeves rolled up for work they will do fine. They will also know that they are on the cutting edge of charity and all the good it does in our world.

Chapter 24 Competition

"Win or lose, do it fairly."

Knute Rockne (college football coach)

Fund raising is a friendly field. This might seem odd, as it could be argued that we are all after the same donors. If a donor gives to your charity he has less to give to mine. It could be a cutthroat, dog eat dog, line of work. It isn't, and that says something important about the people in the profession and about the nature of charity itself.

There are in America today about a dozen national organizations devoted in whole or in part to some aspect of fundraising. A large part of the profession belongs to one or more of these organizations. One of the largest is the Association of Fundraising Professionals (AFP), with chapters in most cities and several other countries. Meetings are generally monthly and members attend to hear speakers address issues related to the job. At a typical luncheon meeting it is not unusual to arrive, spot a table with an empty seat, and join eight or ten people you may or may not know. During the meal, it is common to make introductions, and spend the time before the speaker begins, talking shop with people, who will often represent a wide variety of charities in the area.

It is not uncommon at such gatherings to have a newcomer to the field sitting at the table. This may be someone just starting a job, or a person looking for work and trying to decide if fundraising is for them. Generally, they will be encouraged and given suggestions as to contacts and to where they can apply. I am not saying jobs are easy to find, but unlike some lines of work, the people in fundraising tend to encourage newcomers and wish them well. Many chapters of AFP have standing committees to supply people who are new on the job with a volunteer mentor. This will be someone with experience in the field, who can be called upon for advice. They can also just ask advice from the people they happen to be sitting with at the meeting and often get all the help they need.

I have sat at numerous lunches where someone has asked for ideas and recommendations to help them in their fundraising and the outpouring of information is instantaneous and completely unrestrained. A newcomer may ask about how to organize a special event, where to purchase reasonably priced fundraising software, how to put together a mass mailing or any number of other topics. At one time I was looking for some software to keep track of my donors. One of the people at lunch said her agency had bought a new software program but they still had their old program back at the office and if I wanted it they would give it to me. This was very helpful and allowed us to avoid an expense that would have been the equivalent of a year's salary for a staff person. When I wanted to put on my first golf tournament, the head of a nearby agency spent half the morning showing me all the information she had acquired over years of putting on golf fundraisers. By following exactly what she recommended we started an annual golf tournament that has raised more money than any other event we do. These were acts of pure generosity, by busy people who had no obligation to help me and were my competition in the begging game. I have been happy to do the same for others. I cannot count the number of times someone at an AFP lunch has asked if they could call or come by the office to get some advice on fundraising. I consider it both my duty and pleasure to respond. Most professional fundraisers, that I know, have a similar attitude.

This access to free advice is particularly valuable because the begging game is generally upside-down. In most professions when you are new, you start by learning one aspect of the field and later, as you master more, you advance in the profession. In some cases such as at large national charities or colleges and universities, that pattern still applies. They have large staffs to guide and train a newcomer. However, most charities have small development staffs. Newcomers generally land jobs with small charities because the small ones cannot afford more experienced professionals. This situation means that they must do everything. In a one man shop, one person maintains the donor database, writes the appeals and acknowledgements, plans and executes the special events, recruits and supervises the volunteers, and reports all this directly to the board and the agency director. Beggars start off as a generalists and later move to a larger institution, where they can focus on the aspect of fundraising that they like most. Yet, many in the field remain generalists their entire careers. It can be exciting to do it all. Nonetheless, in the first few months of work, having a friendly professional who will give free advice and guidance is priceless. Not all feel as warmly about their beginning experiences in the field as I do, but there is not the resentment, hazing or ostracism that greets people breaking into other lines of work.

The fact that so many people in the business received that same degree of genuine, selfless help when they were getting started is one reason the beggar game is so friendly and supportive. We owe a debt to those who helped us and we repay it by assisting the newcomers.

But there is also more to this attitude than tradition. Primarily, people go into charity work because they are caring. I cannot overstate that the hours are too long, the pay is too poor, and the responsibility too heavy to appeal to people who don't care about the cause. Besides, if someone works with volunteers and donors, who are donating their time and money, and that staff person's interests are completely selfish and materialistic, they are going to have problems. The degree of hypocrisy between one's professional life and one's personal values will confront them on a daily basis. This dichotomy will bother most people even if they have the sensitivity of a brick. The job just will not meet their needs and vice versa.

This is not to say that beggars are perfect. As with any profession, we get some that are greedy, nasty, lazy, and even crooked. We get our share of stories of vice, theft and corruption. But the vast majority of people in charity work are charitable people.

That charitable nature is one reason for the lack of cutthroat competition for donors. We do not want each other's money. We want the money that would otherwise be goes to yachts, mansions, limousines, jewelry and all the other symbols of worldly materialism. We much prefer the money that is being wasted or hoarded instead of doing good. To take money from each other will not improve things. Beggars raising money for eradicating disease, educating the young, caring for the poor, protecting the environment, spreading art and culture or any other worthwhile cause makes the world better. We beggars want all charities to prosper. New or old, big or little, let all our begging competitors win. If they do, there will be no losers.

Chapter 25 The Post Office

"He pasted a sheet of postage stamps
from snout clear down to tail,
Put on a quick delivery stamp
and sent the cod by mail."
Cure for Homesickness
Francis Day Holman (poet)

Now I will examine that age-old question which burns in the mind of everyone in development and even in the regular business world. How does one entice people to open the envelope and read the mass mailing? A person can write the most appealing and heart rending request in the world, but it won't matter because most such letters will hit the wastebasket unopened and unread.

You have undoubtedly seen numerous ideas used by various companies to get a larger percentage of their envelopes opened, including clever phrases and pictures on the outside or wild hints that there is some treasure inside. You may have seen advertisements disguised as bills, personal letters, tax notices, telegrams and paychecks, just to get you to peek inside before tossing. These devices are all part of the never-ending battle to get you to read the sender's mail.

One reason for all this weird behavior is the post office. The post office wants people to mail things. That is why they are in business. To maximize the use of their automated systems, thus reducing their manpower expenses and increasing profits, the post office offers businesses and charities deals. The post office insures an advertisement will be sent directly to those targeted people, the company sending out the mailer, thinks might be interested. Direct mail is much more focused than TV or radio, where a company pays to send out their message to everyone and hopes the interested people are tuned in. If a charity sends out enough mail, at once, the post office will give the charity a price break. These days, a bulk mail letter can be sent for between one-fourth and one-third the price of a single first class letter. In a world where everyone is not yet using email, it is very cost-effective. For example, a mass mailing requires a lot less staff time and effort than organizing and putting on a special event. Besides, you can request non-deliverable mail be returned and avoid future mailings to bad addresses.

This is not an essay on mass mailing but an examination of the general craziness that goes on in development offices and people's homes over a letter in a mailbox. I have already mentioned the strange tricks I and others think up to get the public to open the envelope. These fads come and go and recently the same sorts of teasers (clever words on the outside) are being used by spammers to get their emails opened. The public has figured out that a letter with a mass mail stamp in the corner and a printed label with their name and address is not a love letter from their sweetheart but just a chance to send money to a stranger. For most people its one quick glance and into the trash. If the general public had an idea of the research, articles, sales campaigns, professional disputes and money that is poured into the issue of getting an envelope torn open, they would be sure we are all crazy.

On the other hand, there is some insanity in the American home. For one thing, who is Occupant and why is his mail always coming to your house? Even when you move you will still get his mail. The speed with which Occupant's mail gets tossed is the reason charities try to have the correct name and address. I say "try to" because we get things wrong sometimes and this is often the place where Mr. and Mrs. America go nuts. A person's name is very important to them, yet even if your name is Smith, you will sooner or later get mail that has your name wrong. In the average charity, staff or volunteers correct the information on people's addresses as they move. The average American moves every seven years, so at any one time, if we send out a mailing of 10,000 letters we will get several hundred undeliverable letters back. Sooner or later, someone typing in that information makes a mistake and "Joe Smith" becomes "Joan Mith". If the person is really tired "Joe Smith" may become "J7^ #+Lth". The odd thing is Joe is often more angry over the gender change than if he is when converted into a space alien named J7^. What is crazy is the number of people who think this sort of thing is done on purpose, as some low joke. Charities are too poor for that kind of humor.

On a related note, proper salutations become even more challenging when addressing women. In a salutation, to a woman, you cannot always safely fall back on "Ms." Older women and especially widows can get very upset if you change "Mrs." to "Ms." The younger generation expects "Ms.", and it is sometimes worth a beggar's life to use "Mrs." or worse "Miss." Over the years, I have been fiercely attacked by both groups for getting it wrong. This is easy to do because when we get someone's name and address, the salutation is generally not included. Members of both groups have agreed that these mistakes undoubtedly occurred because I am an insensitive cloddish male. The fact that this is true is beside the point. Women do most of the data entry where I work, and they don't have a good answer to this issue either.

In conclusion I can only say, "Please open the envelope Mr. and Miss. America. We in the charity world really do have a worthwhile story to tell, and you and your lovely wife J7^ just might find a cause you want to help."

Chapter 26 Prescription for Life

"He who will live for others shall have great troubles,
but they shall seem to him small.
He who will live for himself shall have small troubles,
but they shall seem to him great."
William R. Inge (playwright and novelist)

"Charity is the best way for you to take care of yourself." "If you are involved with the problems of others you do not have the time or energy to worry about your own problems." These clichés are not guaranteed to work. I have often had my eyes pop open at three in the morning worrying about a problem at work. Generally the problem is a variation on the theme of how am I going to raise enough money to allow the agency to continue to help those in need. I know that anxiety is not healthy, nor does it put a penny in our bank account, but I still fall victim to it. I also know it is not a good Christian habit. Saint John Vianny, the bishop of Ars France during the nineteenth centaury pointed out that "God commands us to pray, but forbids us to worry." I understand that my anxiety is a useless, self-inflicted wound but my eyes still pop open at three AM.

Yet, I still think the words of William Inge are true and I have seen those words play out often in life. My godfather was a medical missionary. Dr. Billy Rodgers Beasley worked many years in Africa, later in India and finally in the hills of rural Kentucky. I doubt that I saw him more than eight or nine occasions during my entire life. Yet, his life exerted a positive influence on me that I still sense today. When I was about five or six, he sent me a carved wooden mask from Liberia as a gift. It has been with me ever since and hangs on my living-room wall today. The last time I saw him, he and his wife had retired to the college town of Sewanee Tennessee where he had studied many years before. There was the sort of relaxed warmth in the visit, which generally only occurs when old friends gather. These people had spent their lives taking a deep personal interest in others. While the house was filled with mementos of their life and they were now retired, very little of the conversation was about the past. Much of the conversation, when not focused on me or my son (who was traveling with me) was about current projects they were involved with. It was very clear they were not vegetating. It was an extremely pleasant visit and I was sorry it only lasted two days.

When my godfather died, there was a memorial service in the Episcopal Church he and I had both grown up in. People came from all over, and it was one of the warmest and lighthearted funerals I have attended. People felt good about knowing Dr. Billy Rodgers Beasley.

By the world's standards he had not done very well. He had passed up a chance to be a rich doctor in a modern American hospital and had moved his wife and children off to places of poverty, disease, and downright danger. He had failed to become either rich or famous. All he had was the gratitude of people who generally could not afford to pay him. Yet I feel the title of godson to Dr. Beasley ranks as one of the greatest honors of my life.

At the end of the service the congregation sang a hymn that used to be in the children's section of the Episcopal hymnal when I was in the youth choir. The song was written in 1929 by Lesbia Scott and could stand as the theme song for all people who do charity work. To have such a song sung at his funeral seemed completely appropriate. His was as strong and spiritually healthy a life as anyone could ask for.

I sing a song of the saints of God
Patient and brave and true.
Who toiled and fought and lived and died
For the Lord they loved and knew.
And one was a doctor, and one was a queen,
And one was a shepherdess on the green:
They were all of them saints of God-and I mean,
God helping to be one too.

They loved their Lord so dear, so dear,
And his love made them strong;
And they followed the right, for Jesus sake,
The whole of their good lives long.

And one was a soldier, and one was a priest,
And one was slain by a fierce wild beast:
And there's not any reason-no, not the least-
Why I shouldn't be one too.

They lived not only in ages past,
There are hundreds of thousands still,
The world is bright with joyous saints
Who love to do Jesus' will.
You can meet them in school, or in lanes, or at sea,
In church, or in trains, or in shops, or at tea,
For the saints of God are just folk like me,
And I mean to be one too.

Chapter 27 Special Events

"He is truly great who hath a great charity."

Imitation of Christ

Thomas a Kempis (Renaissance era monk)

My agency just finished a "special event". A special event is a less obvious way to beg for money. A street musician, with his instrument case open for money while he plays, is holding a special event. Charities hold all sorts of special events to raise money or to honor and thank donors and volunteers.

Putting on special events is not my strong suit even though it has been a major part of my job. I have never been one for hosting parties. I do not enjoy the planning, decorating and everything else that goes with a big party. However, this is just a personal bias and many other people do enjoy it. I have been fortunate and grateful to have had such people on my event planning committees.

The whole idea in development is that people will give you something for nothing. You have a charity. You may feed the poor, cure disease, educate the young, protect stray animals or any number of things. Our world generally understands these are good things to do even if we do not receive direct benefits from them.

Any good encyclopedia of ethics and morals (try larger libraries or the internet) will show people from all over the world with all sorts of faiths share many of the same values of the hearth. Mercy is better than justice, murder is wrong, deceiving or cheating those close to you is bad and so on. Various cultures may put different spins on these rules, but they exist everywhere humans have lived and developed in community. They used to be what was meant by "natural law" and were understood to be as universal and natural as gravity.

Thus we can say that our world buys into the value of these things. However, when it comes to paying for them, the support drops way off. The old expression "give till it hurts" finds most people in pain if they even touch their purse much less open it. This is understandable, because in the charity world, you give twenty five thousand dollars and we will put your name on a plaque. For the same money, General Motors will provide you with a new car! You get a much better return on your material investment in the material world.

Therefore charities must try to make giving as painless as possible. Special events let donors have some fun and see other people giving so they don't feel they are alone in their giving decision. Still it is hard because they know that they can play golf somewhere else for less money than in our tournament or eat a nice dinner for less than the charity banquet charges.

There is also the problem of the charity's image. This is a particular difficulty for me because my charity helps poor people. If our event looks too nice or our appeal mailing looks too fancy we will be strongly criticized by people who do not want their money "wasted" when it could be helping the poor. Any money spent on administration, or more especially on fund raising is viewed by some, as money "wasted".

Church members can be the most critical on the issue of "too fancy". Many stalwart supporters on limited incomes do not understand that wealthy people expect more for dinner than tuna casserole, served while sitting on metal folding chairs, in a church basement. If that is what we offer to the people who can write the big checks, such people may come if they are loyal, but they will not invite their friends. The business concept that "you have to spend money to make money" goes against many church members' view of giving in humble appreciation of God's blessings. The church people are, of course, completely correct. Thus the development staff must work creatively to tailor events to match the different needs and attitudes of different donor groups.

Still, things can get ugly. A few years ago we put together an appeal and an information mass mailing. We were trying to renovate the building and we needed more money than ever. We tried a new concept and sent a copy of a short video to each of our donors. Other people had used this technique very effectively and we had great hopes. It did not do well and several people called me concerned about the cost. I explained we had gotten much of the work underwritten and the cost was about that of a normal mailing.

One woman wrote me to say she had thrown the video in the trash the moment it arrived and would never send another penny to an organization that wasted money in such a way. She said she had sent her money to "empower the poor" not to waste it on fundraising. I wrote back saying I was sorry she felt that way and explained about keeping the cost as low as we could. I never heard back from her. She and her husband were new donors who had given a first donation check of $200 about three months before. At the time I was hurt and angry but now I view it as one of the risks that comes with a "one size fits all" funding program. The restraints of time and budget can cause beggars to offend.

You never know what will die in one place and fly in another. Several months later we were trying to get a donation from a wealthy businessman. We wanted him to see the agency but he was unable to work it into his schedule. In comparison to some of his causes ours was fairly small and unimportant. We knew that people who actually saw the program in action were much more likely to give than those who just heard about it second hand. We feared that without some form of direct contact this donor was not likely to do very much if anything. We sent him printed information and a copy of the video. We hoped he would take 10 minutes out of his day to watch the video. The next day he called me, saying he had watched the video and would be sending us a donation. The amount he sent was the largest single gift any individual had given our agency in its entire 100 year history. That single gift paid the expenses of making and mailing the video many times over. It allowed us to meet all our budget needs for the year. For him, that 10 minute presentation was exactly what he needed to make his decision.

The beggar must tailor the solicitation to the donor. For some people time is more important than money. For others the donation may need to fill some preconceived idea of helping. Others may need a certain type of recognition to feel their gift is worthwhile. The beggar's confidence that the gift will be "put to good use" is not enough. People can be very demanding about "their money".

Chapter 28 The Fear of Begging

"Courage is doing what you're afraid to do.
There can be no courage unless you're scared."
Eddie Rickenbacker (World War I ace aviator)

"I hate asking people for money!" "I will be happy to volunteer but I don't want to ask for money." "Please don't ask me to be on the endowment committee. I am not comfortable asking people for a donation." "Yes, I will go with you to meet with her about the campaign, but don't expect me to do the asking."

These statements are common in fundraising. As professionals, we encounter resistance all the time. Most people are uncomfortable asking others for money. I have had people say, "I will give you a check myself, just don't ask me to ask other people." They will do anything to avoid asking others for money. They may fear rejection or conversely fear a reciprocal gift request from the donor if they succeed. I remember my attempt to recruit an executive with a major corporation as a fundraiser. He had helped other charities in the past get donations and I wanted him helping us solicit some large donations. His refusal was quite clear. "Every time I asked my friends to donate to my favorite charities they then turned around and insisted I give to their favorite. I wound up giving more than I wanted to all sorts of causes I was not interested in, so now I never ask others for donations."

This is not universally true, and the issues of fear of rejection and reciprocal obligations have solutions. (Making the charity the issue rather than doing a personal favor helps with reciprocity.) Almost anyone can be made into a successful fundraiser, given the right training and support. Experts in the beggar game know the basic rules of how to make a shy, nervous volunteer into a confident, successful fundraiser. They know to take them along on a well-planned visit to a prospect. They know to get them to tell about their interest and love of the cause. They know to teach them that the word "no" is not something to fear, or even to pay much attention to.

As I have mentioned before that there is a philosophy in the profession that says, "We do not beg". Development professionals are supposed to point out the good work the charity does, and how the donor can help, and allow them to respond. However, if the people respond with nothing more than a cheer and a round of applause the beggar has received a response that pays no bills. Newspaper columnists, politicians and other public figures are often heard praising some charity or another for its good work; this praise does not mean they will contribute a dime. Praise is cheaper than cash. If a charity wants money it has to ask. Only the IRS does not have to ask. They demand you support the fine work done by our glorious nation. As I pointed out in another chapter, to turn your back on their demands will land you in jail. Even so, most citizens would rather cheer for America than pay for it. I remember the great radio announcer, Arthur

Godfrey, once said, "I'm proud to pay taxes in the United States; the only thing is, I could be just as proud for half the money." Thus the IRS never asks, it insists.

We have to ask, and this is very hard for most people. Some feel it is shameful to be weak and need help. Some feel panic when confronted with the role of public spokesperson. They dislike being the focus of attention. As I mentioned, many fear failure. They don't want to be turned down and fail the cause they love. All of these concerns are about leaving behind one's own comfort zone. All of them are about fear.

In his great work "The Road Less Traveled", Scott Peck describes sloth as the worst of the seven deadly sins. When he is talking about sloth, he is not describing it as indolence or laziness but as reluctance or refusal to grow and change. He maintains that the basis for this reluctance is fear. Resistance to change and growth is an aspect of fear of the unknown. Fear of the unknown is the most universal terror of all.

Children suffer from it when they begin to be uncomfortable around strangers. We fear death because death is the greatest unknown in human existence. Growth is change and change places us in the unknown.

And yet sloth is identified by many as a sin and not a normal condition. The reason sloth is seen as a sin is that growth is an essential part of life. A baby that does not emerge from the womb will die. Change is the one great universal constant of God's creation. To reject change is to reject all creation. We see this in the psychology of people who stop growing at some point or another. Such terms as spoiled, immature, arrested development, Peter Pan complex, or old fogies are never compliments and yet, to grow requires courage. The term "growing pains" is a legitimate description. We do not fear the unknown without reason. The courage to live life is not easy and, as Peck points out, it gets harder to keep growing and changing as we get older. It is often love that acts as the catalyst to give us the courage to continue to grow. In fund raising, we often see the phenomena of a shy tongue-tied person becoming very articulate and animated as they speak of the cause they love.

This outburst of eloquence by a shy person is the great moment. You might not think so, but it is. We are happy the person gets so excited and the prospect writes a big check. Afterwards, the volunteer beggar is amazed he was able to say all he did and we are happy everything went well. If we really pay attention we see so much more, for this is the moment when love lights courage and courage makes a new man. This is when a middle-aged housewife becomes the new Sir Galahad in shining armor. This is the moment when a retired accountant becomes Joan of Arc. This is a truck driver picking up the cloak of Elijah. This is the fire from Heaven. The miracle of Pentecost is described in Acts 2, as when the apostles received the Holy Spirit, like tongues of flame and were suddenly able to speak many languages. That type of miracle need not be just Bible history.

Chapter 29 Giving Thanks

"Gratitude is not only the greatest of virtues, but the parent of all others."

Marcus Tullius Cicero (Roman statesman)

A saying in the world of fundraising states that we are to thank donors at least seven times. That may sound like a lot but it is about right. When someone donates, the charity should send the donor a receipt. The letter can both start and end with a word of thanks. The middle can be a promise to use the money well. The whole letter need not be more than three or four lines long. My charity also has staff or volunteers call and say thanks. They spend most of their time talking to answering machines, but people do like the personal touch and we have learned that donors will tell us more about themselves and their reasons for donating in these phone conversations. Again, a volunteer for the charity can start by explaining who they are and that the reason for their call is to express thanks. They can end the call with a simple "thanks again" as the closing. Also, one can show appreciation by listing donor's names in newsletters, annual reports, honor rolls, and other public listings of friends and supporters. With letters, emails, phone calls, personal contacts and various types of listings reaching seven is not that difficult, even for modest gifts. With larger gifts it gets even easier.

On phone calls, I cannot over emphasize how much donors appreciate a chance to talk with a representative of the charity. For years we have had two retires calling from their homes. The second man was a regular donor and when he began receiving a call as well as a letter for each gift he was so impressed with the program he agreed to phone all the out of town donors from his home and absorb the long distance cost himself. He made a point of learning when the donors were coming to town and arranging special tours of the agency for them. He has become one of the agency's best ambassadors.

The man who makes our local phone calls has been in charity work all his adult life. He is well known and well respected in the community and a large number of our donors look forward to a call from him. Our policy is to make a call on every gift, no matter how small. Donors are often stunned to get a personal call for a five dollar gift but we believe that small donors are an essential part of our strength and we want them to know it. This system has allowed us to build up a long term personal relationship with some very kind and generous people. Not long ago our local caller informed me that he had just thanked a lady for her gift. Previously, the lady was a major supporter of other charities but her donations to us had been modest. The lady informed our caller that she had such a positive impression of the agency from his calls that she would not only increase her gifts but would include us in her estate plans. People appreciate personal thanks.

Showing appreciation to donors is a basic truism of the job. Yet it is often ignored, and sometimes by large charitable institutions who ought to know better. I have repeatedly heard donors complain about well respected charities that send out another appeal instead of an appreciation letter after a donation. The professionals, who run such campaigns, will quote all sorts of mailing savings for not bothering with thanks. They will talk of the dollars that come from the appeal letters triggered by donations. They will refuse to realize that people are giving in spite of their tactics, not because of them.

On a practical level, I could talk about the fact that not thanking donors, sooner or later, results in some other cause wooing them away. People will go, and take their money where they are appreciated. I could even point out that keeping and nurturing donors is much less expensive that finding new ones. Running off donors is about the most expensive mistake a beggar can make.

Charities have a real need to thank donors. Thanking people is not a duty it is an honor. Thanking people is a joy filled delight. Thanking people is laying a blessing on them. In our harsh world it is the annunciation of salvation. That donor is a healer, that donor is a protector, that donor is a teacher and that donor is a builder. All that a cause does is because of that donor.

Many of us can be embarrassed by thanks. We often dismiss thanks with such phrases as "it was nothing," or "no need to thank me," or "forget it," when offered thanks. But remember, we were generally taught, as children, that the response to thanks is "you are welcome". This is important, because "welcome" is an invitation in. As a bringer of thanks and deserved praise you are a legitimately welcome guest in another's life. To dismiss thanks is not noble or selfless, but very sad. If God's Holy Spirit has been moved through you to do a good deed you need to stand open to the dose of healing salve for your soul that thanks can give. We will get plenty of unwelcome heralds announcing the world's condemnation of us. So take the blessings when they come. They are a unique form of refreshment.

I offer this challenge to all Development Directors not interested in thanking people. We in Development have no better reason to exist than offering thanks. Never mind the special events, the annual campaigns, the budget, or even the cause. Those things will sort themselves out. We are conveying the salvation of praise. We exist to carry blessings to those who have lifted themselves out of themselves, to place one grain of sand in the building of a better world. If they reject the blessing, or don't recognize it for what it is, that is not our problem. Our job is to deliver the good news that they have changed the world for the better.

I enjoy thanking people. I get a great kick out of it. It is quite amusing to contact someone, and watch them slowly come out of their defensive shell as they realize that I am only going to thank them, and it is not a ploy to ask for more money. This is especially true when phoning people because we have become so conditioned to phone calls from strangers being a sales pitch. People tend to be defensive on the phone, because there are so many phone solicitors with fake friendly voices. Generally they will hear me out in silence, until I am saying goodbye, and then they realize that it is not a sales call. Suddenly, there is a great sigh of relief and the words start pouring out of them. They become very friendly and relaxed, and I often have a nice chat. I would consider it a kind of betrayal of trust to ask for anything at that point. I am there to deliver the blessing. It lifts me out of myself too. It is a direct contact with a person I know to be charitable. Who better to commune with?

So, fellow beggars of the world unite! Thank those donors, again and again, over and over. We are involved in a transcendental experience. Besides, they need the receipt for tax purposes.

Chapter 30 Death and Charity

"What the caterpillar calls the end of the world, the master calls a butterfly."

Matthew Arnold (English poet)

A close friend of mine lost her mother over the weekend. We are often confronted with death, and it seems there is little to do when it happens. However, the reality is there is a great deal that must be done. Endings require change for everyone who was involved with whatever ended. Death removes someone we were directly or indirectly involved with. For anyone who loses someone close, the change can be a permanently debilitating one, like an amputation. The wound heals and the pain will decrease until it is only an occasional twinge. Still, the missing limb stays gone. You may get a prosthetic limb, and lead a full and active life, but it is not the same as having your arm or leg back. The deceased parent, sibling, child, or friend that is gone was unique and your relationship with them cannot be duplicated. With their death you are changed and from that change there is no going back.

Death plays a large role in the charity world. I am not talking about wills and bequests. That has to do with something decided by the departed, while they were still alive. I am speaking of the response people have to death, and to some of the other great losses of life. Divorce, bankruptcy, job loss, even relocation can and do create traumatic and permanent change in people. None of these have the complete finality of death, but they do turn people's lives upside down, and may shatter the recipient. Still, the death of a loved one is the main event which turns people toward charity.

A child dies of an incurable disease and the parents spend the rest of their lives fighting for a cure. One youngster was killed by a drunk driver and soon a mother's dedication to ending such tragedy resulted in Mothers Against Drunk Driving (MADD) as a national crusade. Charity after charity has been started, enriched and driven by people who wanted to do something to prevent others going through the loss they endured. It is impossible to measure the medical, social and political change from people galvanized into action by death.

Not long after the 9-11 tragedy, more than one writer pointed out that the outpouring of help and concern seemed to provide equilibrium to the tragedy. The millions of small acts of kindness and concern were the response to the great evil of a few. More recently, the 2004 Tsunami in the Indian Ocean resulted in the entire world making a rapid and concerted effort to help. Sudden violent death seems to trigger charity as nothing else.

I don't mean to say that the aid sent to the families makes up for their loss or even that the world is getting better. Modern man is still just as violent, lazy, self-centered, greedy and foolish as his Bronze Age ancestors. (If you doubt this add up the millions of war dead in the twentieth centaury then add to it all the millions killed by governments in the gulags, gas chambers, killing fields and other modern forms of mass murder.) Charity can only be seen as evidence he is not getting worse.

Many people get involved in charities because the cause mattered to their loved ones. Often, it is a way of continuing something that was important to the departed. This is charity as a tradition and allows the donor or volunteers to keep alive the memory of some noble and generous aspect of their loved one. I have heard someone say, "Mother always loved flowers, so volunteering at the Botanical Garden makes me feel close to her".

Anna Jarvis spent much of her life creating Mother's Day because of the loss of her own mother. This one woman worked tirelessly to establish a holiday to honor mothers everywhere. She managed to get it established as a national holiday by President Wilson and she had the first celebration on the date of her own mother's death. She even started the tradition of giving carnations on Mother's Day because it was her mother's favorite flower. This is just one example of the force stirred up in a person due to the death of a loved one.

Finally, it is important to understand that charity fights against death. This fight is of central importance because being alive is the only reality we know. Through charity we fight against the tools of death. All those things that kill us include not just disease or accident, but hate, violence, hunger, ignorance and indifference. Charity is about love and love makes war on all these things. This fight against the tools of death is a fight that will last all our lives and we will see many setbacks and defeats. However, engaging in this fight is seen by people of many faiths as a victory in itself. For most of the people on the planet their faith tells them that their love in this life plays a role in their experience of another life.

Chapter 31 Open Wide Your Hand

"The appearance of things change according to the emotions and thus we see magic and beauty in them, while the magic and beauty are really in ourselves."
Kahlil Gilbran (poet)

A few years ago I needed a new slogan for our annual campaign. There are many verses in the Bible about money and giving. Many in the New Testament have been used so often that they were never going to seem unique to our campaign. In Deuteronomy I found just what I needed. "For the poor will never cease out of the land; therefore I command you, 'You shall open wide your hand to your brother, to the needy and to the poor in the land.'"[Deut. 15:11.] While this quotation is used frequently, it was not as familiar to my donors as some of the others and it had a wonderful visual image. We have used it for a number of years now and have maintained good steady growth.

Even after all this usage, the verse still holds a strong message about giving for me. A closed fist is never seen as a generous or friendly image. A fist is an accepted sign of anger or tension. An open hand is relaxed. It requires tension to hold something in our hand. If the object has any weight it will slip out if we do not grip it. We generally want to hold on tightly to those things we value and consider ours. As small children when our parents would give us money to buy something, we learned to hold tight to a coin until we made the purchase. We learned very early that a dropped quarter could roll away and be lost.

But if we believe that God created the universe then what can we grip that is not God's already? The very fingerprints that mark our unique natures and whose uneven ridges aid our grip are God's workmanship. The closed, grasping hand that holds our worldly treasures must open, and risk things falling out. As the hand opens and risks loss, it is also open to receive gifts. God does not place gifts in closed fists.

Another example of God recommending risk is shown in the Bible verse, Ecclesiastes 11:1: "Cast your bread upon the waters, for after many days you will find it again…" Farmers know that if you eat all your grain you will starve after one harvest. The ancient farmers went out in small flat boats on the river as the water was receding from the spring floods, and scattered the seed grain on the shallow water. It was risky, because if they went too soon after the spring floods, the strong water would wash the grain away. If they waited too long the water would be gone and the seeds could not sink into the soft mud to germinate or the hot summer sun would burn up the young seedling plants before they could grow. Only in risking the last of their good bread grain, by tossing it into the water, could they produce a new crop.

Giving can always be perceived as risky. These days there is much talk of donors demanding greater accountability and input as to the use of their money. However, if charity only helps those where there is certainty of positive results, most in need will not be helped. Under measurable, positive, results guidelines, Mother Teresa's mission in Calcutta would have never received a single donation. Her clients generally died! She was helping poor, dying beggars and most were not going to recover. This is hardly a good track record of results. Yet she is exactly the sort of gift the writer of Ecclesiastes is speaking of. Mother Teresa poured out love and care on people she was unlikely to save as an act of faith. She realized her patients would generally not recover but she was determined to help the most unfortunate. Her life became an inspiration to the world!

The world has many good hearted, socially concerned, and civic-minded, atheists and agnostics. I understand that for them the issues may be different. They can legitimately feel they must be careful with their money. Their view of life may mean they need to see results here and now. The atheist often needs to believe in human progress or give knowing the gift changes nothing in a meaningless world. If they are cheated, and their money is wasted, it is a complete loss. However, the followers of God receive no indication that their charity on earth will change anything. The people of God are told to help others as an act of worship. This can be seen in several places in the Bible including Proverbs 19:17 "He that hath mercy on the poor, lendeth to the Lord: and he will repay him." (Douay-Rheims Translation), Luke 14:13-14 "But when thou makest a feast, call the poor, the maimed, the lame, the blind: And thou shalt be blessed; for they cannot recompense thee: for thou shalt be recompensed at the resurrection of the just." (King James Version) and Acts 20:35 "In all things I gave you an example, that so laboring ye ought to help the weak, and to remember the words of the Lord Jesus, that he himself said, It is more blessed to give than to receive." (American Standard Version) Any wrong use of the time or money donated by the faithful does not reflect against them, but on those who misused it.

This does not imply that the faithful are not called to prudence. Prudence is a great virtue and it seems to be a reasonable assumption that God put our brains in our heads for a reason. My point is that the servant of God may trust in God, and while hurt by the waste of his gifts, need not be ashamed or worse, cynical. He may sleep with good conscience, for he has opened wide his hand, and that is all God asks.

Chapter 32 Grants

"The philosophers have only interpreted the world in various ways. The point, however, is to change it."
Karl Marx (German philosopher and revolutionary)

Whenever professional beggars gather for seminars and meetings, the topic of grant writing always draws a crowd. In the overall world of charitable giving in America, the financial grants of foundations are a small piece of the pie, only 11.6% in 2004. However, this money still manages to attract the beggars and the reason is simple. Grants can be for very large sums of money, (even millions of dollars) from a source you do not have to spend years building up support and interest from. No big special event, no expensive mass mailing is required just one staff person responsible for putting a written proposal in the mail. What could be easier? Small new charities have the same chance as large established ones of having their requests funded. Just convince the foundation of the worthwhile nature of your idea and the money is yours. Loyalty and familiarity play only a small role in this arena.

A charity may need money for a project that it cannot reasonably expect to get from its regular donors. Charities understand that just because they have supporters, does not mean they can get big bucks from their donors, just because the charity has needs. In America, religion gets the biggest piece of the donation pie (35.5% in 2004). Yet the local church cannot realistically expect $50,000 checks in the collection plate every Sunday. The famous comedian, Milton Berle once told the following story:

In the vault where the U. S. Treasury Department keeps old worn out paper currency, two of the bills were talking. A hundred-dollar bill said, "I've had some life—the best restaurants, the finest shops. How about you?" A one-dollar bill said, "It has been very boring. All I ever did was go to church, go to church, go to church."

Thus it follows that if you have limited time and resources for your project, no matter how worthy, a grant from a foundation may be your best bet. Yet, there is a very real downside to grant writing that foundations often ignore, and charities, out of fear of offending the foundations, don't want to talk about. Just because you apply does not mean you get the money.

I am not talking about the ways a charity can insure it will get turned down by acting foolishly and ignoring the foundation's application guidelines. Foundations become legitimately angry with charities that act in an unprofessional way. I have listened to staff from foundations complain about charities asking for money for projects that are clearly not something the foundation funds. People will ask for money to build a park from a foundation that only funds medical research. One staff person told me her board meets twice a year to make decisions about grants. The date of the meeting is posted on their web site and on all the information they send out, but every year she will get applications one or two days after the meeting is over and these will be followed up by angry phone calls from the charity wanting to know why they were not funded. It is not surprising that a foundation is reluctant to supply money to a charity that demonstrates its staff is either too lazy or stupid to read and follow the guidelines. Yet charities that follow all the rules and meet all the deadlines may still go unfunded.

Now everyone is accustomed to getting requests for donations in the mail from charities they do not support. People are under no obligation to donate and most toss these appeals in the trash, without further notice. However, it is one thing to toss unsolicited donation requests in the trash, and another if someone contacts a charity and asks to be put on the mailing list with no real intention of donating. In this case they are wasting the charity's resources. A fairly large number of foundations actively advertise for grant proposals or encourage submissions from charities that contact them.

Now foundations do make grants, but to research and write a grant proposal is no small undertaking and can keep someone busy for days or weeks. If the foundation generally gives twenty, or even a hundred grants, annually, but routinely gets five hundred to five thousand requests, the vast majority of charities hoping for help are going to be cruelly disappointed. Often, only when the charity gets the turndown form letter does the foundation point out how many more applications they receive than they can honor.

Foundation boards and staff focus on all the good they do and this is fine. They do a great deal of good. Unfortunately the grant system, as it now exists, breaks a lot of hearts. A slightly more realistic response to inquiries, and requests for applications, might be more humane. Something along the lines of, "Don't get your hopes up. We give twenty grants in the average year and we get six hundred requests." This issue may not impact the general public but it does impact the morale of a charity's staff and volunteers.

In bad economic times foundations are much more reluctant to take applications. When there is a downturn in the stock market, foundations have less money to give away. Their resources are tied to the market and they get a smaller dividend to give out. Unfortunately, when the market is down individual giving also drops off as people have less disposable income. This situation throws increasing numbers of charities into the shrinking grant pool as they desperately search for alternative funding. This is not a criticism of foundations, only an explanation of the way the charitable world works.

Still, the bottom line is that foundations make it possible for small understaffed new charities to get a start, and it is never easy to start. A non-profit business is still a business, and the mortality rate in new business is always very high. I owned a business for many years, and I remember that Dun and Bradstreet,

(The company that does most of the credit reports on businesses in America) would not give the business any rating until it was at least seven years old. Dun and Bradstreet rated a business's financial health based on a formula for how well the business was doing and what was the likelihood of it staying open.

What was depressing was that Dun and Bradstreet would not bother to rate a business less than seven years old as "bad" and likely to fail. All businesses less than seven years old were likely to fail! They were uniformly bad risks! I do not know if the rating system has changed, but I do know that to open a business today whether nonprofit or not is still a big risk. So any foundation that will help a new charity shows great courage.

Chapter 33 An Ounce of Prevention

"Do all the good you can, by all the means you can, in all the ways you can, in all the places you can, at all the times you can, to all the people you can, as long as ever you can." John Wesley (religious leader and founder of Methodism)

Not long ago, in my Sunday School, our rector spoke about thinking of "sin" as infection, rather than as a wrongful act. He asked us to use the word "infection" sometime during the week, in this context. After thinking about the matter I realized there was an aspect of this proposition related to charity.

The image of sin as infection is often used today, but the infection image seems to conflict with the traditional concept called cognitive will. Let me explain this as I understand the concept. If you think of sin as an act against God or his creation, the cognitive will aspect of the sin is that you consciously choose to do it. It cannot be an accident or something you are forced to do. An illustration of the idea might be that if you are walking in the woods and the wind causes a dead branch to fall out of a tree and hit your arm, you may be hurt and angry, but you will not come back later and cut the tree down to punish it. Such a step would be silly. You'd know the accident was a bit of bad luck, not a deliberate attack. However, if you are walking down the street and someone deliberately throws a rock at you, your reaction will be different. Even if the person misses, and you escape unharmed you will be angry and offended. You have been wronged as well as attacked. You may call the police and demand the person be arrested. The person chose to endanger you. You will be angrier with the rock thrower who missed than at the tree, whose limb almost broke your arm. The rock thrower has acted with cognitive will while the tree limb falling was a random occurrence of nature. The image of God being angrier at a sinner just thinking about murdering someone, than at a car driver who through no fault of their own, accidentally kills someone in a crash supports the idea of cognitive will as an aspect of sin.

I mentioned the concept that a harmful act is not sin if you are forced to do it. But in his lesson our rector pointed out the problem with sin as deliberate wrongful acts. People often feel they have an excuse for sin and often feel they could not help committing the sinful act. Clergy, who hear confessions, will listen to an endless stream of justifications for sins. They will also hear the phrase, "I just couldn't help myself" or "the Devil made me do it" many times. The last thing anyone wants is to take ownership of his or her wrongs. This self view may have become more common with people today as a side effect of popular psychiatric theories on compulsions. In any case many people do think their actions can all be justified in some way. What does it help to tell someone they have done wrong if they are convinced they had no choice?

In his book "Murder Incorporated" Bertram Turkas spoke about how the contract killers for the syndicate always referred to their victims as "Da Bum". By labeling their victims as "bums", the mob assassins allowed themselves a justification for the murder of people they didn't even know. Everyone can use justification to avoid their actions being sins.

If we think of sin as infection we get closer to what many see as God's attitude toward it and toward us. God wants sin gone. He knows how dangerous and how all pervasive it is. But, just as a mother will not be angry with a child when the child has the flu, so God will not punish us when we are infected. The mother may wish the child had washed his hands more often, and not gone to play with his sick friend but first she wants he child well. God wants us well but the cure can sometimes be painful. I will illustrate this with a personal experience.

When I was about four years old I was very badly burned. My mother was in another room when I decided to try my hand at cooking. I filled a large pot with water, added all the sugar in the sugar bowl and put this mixture on the stove. When it started to boil over, I decided it was done and attempted to set it near the kitchen window to cool. In the process, the hot pot slipped from my hands and I poured the entire contents on myself. My soaked clothing held the boiling liquid firmly against my body and I received third degree burns over my stomach, thigh and leg. In an instant I entered a Hell of pain, and remained there for the next several weeks.

I remember little of the rush to the emergency room, or of my stay in the hospital. What was etched into my psyche forever was the ritual of changing the dressings. In those days, they were still using bandages covered with yellow ointment to reduce the sticking of the bandage to the wound. Unfortunately, they did stick and had to be pulled free. There was no way of anesthetizing the wound, because the doctors had to know if the tissue was alive or dead, and cut away the dead tissue. Sometimes they cut live tissue. As the treatment went on, my skin began to heal and the need to change the bandages became less frequent. None of this changed what was going on in my mind. I was terrified of the pain and I was incapable of being rational about it.

Whenever the doctor would enter my room or later when my parents took me to the hospital as an outpatient, I would always start asking if he was going to change the bandages. Sometimes he would say "no" right away and I could calm down a bit. But too many times he would say "yes" or "we'll see" and I began to cry. I would beg him not to. He would examine me and try to be as comforting and reassuring as he could. It made no difference. I would become hysterical and the nurses had to come in and hold me down. They always had the strangest look on their faces. I feared that look worse then death itself because I knew what was going to happen next. Then my doctor would pull off the bandages.

I do not know how many times this was done or how well I was progressing. I only knew there was a giant demon of pain waiting to tear me to pieces because those dressings were stuck to my burned skin and pulling them off tore the wounds. I could not be reasonable, or even understand that the pain was getting less with each changing. I would flip out and begin screaming each time. Remember, I was only four years old.

I am now in my mid-fifties, and have a completely different understanding of what that entire episode meant. I now understand that strange look the nurses had when they held me down. I was looking at sorrow and determination combined. These were dedicated pediatric doctors and nurses. They loved children and hated to see them suffer. My case was written up and helped lead to improved procedures in burn care. Those people were doing their best to help me. But they understood something I did not. Even if they could have explained it to me, it would not have helped back then. Now I know that those bandages were full of germs. If they were not changed my wounds would have become infected and I would have died. They were determined to save my life whether I wanted them to or not. They were going to save me no matter what it cost me, and no matter what it cost them. It must have cost them a lot, because these were committed healers who had devoted their lives to children, and they did not enjoy torturing a small child. In the end, they won their fight for my life. It is half a century later and I am still going strong.

My point in this story is that this is how God sees people. People have gotten infected with a deadly disease called sin that separates them from God and each other. God is going to cure it. Human beings are to spend eternity clean and uninfected. But the cure can sometimes be hard work. Someone who has overcome an addiction through a twelve step program can testify to the hard work involved. We have to spend much of our time scrubbing the infected parts to clean them, and our heavenly doctor has indicated that if amputation is needed, he will do it. Jesus speaks of entering heaven minus an eye or a hand, if it offends. But our doctor will do whatever is necessary to cure us and keep us alive. He is going to change those bandages and clean that infection, no matter what. With this in mind prevention is more desirable than cure.

Now back to charity. Charity is one of Doctor God's best preventatives and treatments of disease. Disease is dis-ease; it is against ease, against good feeling. People, actively involved in helping others, find they feel good. They are focused on others rather than themselves. Over the years, I have talked to so many volunteers who feel great, about what they are doing. Sin is soul sickness, and love for others is both a cure and a preventative. Now, I am no quack doctor selling a patent medicine. I will make no undue claims. Charity will not prevent all spiritual infection nor will it heal every broken heart. Yet it can help prevent the rot of greed, hate, fear and sloth from taking complete control of us.

The old expression was that an ounce of prevention was worth a pound of cure. If a life spent in charitable relations with others can prevent even one of the many desperate and dangerous situations we will face in life from seeming hopeless or uncontrollable it is time well invested. To put our lives back together after we have destroyed it through our fear and despair is much harder work than volunteering to help others. If nothing else, helping others will allow us to learn we live in a world where, when circumstances change, others will help us. That knowledge is a strong defense against despair caused by loneliness. In a charitable world you learn that if you are troubled by feelings of loneliness it does not mean you are really alone. Others love you and you can let them help.

Chapter 34 So You Want to Be a Rock and Roll Star

"Measure twice, cut once."
Traditional Carpenter's Motto

Recently the IRS announced that it had issued the one millionth 501(c)(3) tax designation, the exemption for a charity. Labor unions, professional organizations, political groups and other types of tax exempt entities have other designations in the tax code. There are over a million charities that have met the IRS's rigid standards, to be exempt from federal taxes as they go about the business of doing good in America. That fact makes charity a major player in the American economy.

Everybody seems to want to start his or her own charity these days. Even if you have no interest in starting your own, new charities are a big part of the fund-raising world today and you may feel the effects of it all around you. There are several reasons for this growth.

A number of recent surveys indicate that Americans are more distrustful of their institutions than ever before. While it is true that charities do not suffer from this distrust as much as business or government, there is some distance from donors that was not there fifty years ago. Nowadays it is as common for people to look to solve problems by starting up a new charity as by turning to one of the large traditional charities.

A second reason for the growth in charities is one currently drawing the attention of congress and the IRS, and that is the use of charities as a tax dodge. As long as there have been taxes, there have been people trying to avoid paying them. The government never likes to see money it thinks it has a legitimate claim on getting away. There have been some real abuses recently, but part of the reason that charity scandals make news, is the size and importance of charity itself. Hopefully, once some of the loopholes get closed the interest of the government will drop off. Regrettably, there will always be people ready to start up a charity for their own benefit, rather than for others. Crime goes were money is, and there is money in the world of charity. When asked why he robbed banks, Willie Sutton the famous robber responded, "That's where the money is." People who engage in theft or fraud will use whatever helps them in their crimes and a charity, like any business, can be misused for dishonest profit.

However, there is a third reason for the increase in charities that is a more positive one. Americans are entrepreneurs. They like to take direct action at a problem and they like business ventures. A non-profit business is still a business, and Americans of all social and political backgrounds like trying to help others while being their own boss. If someone starts up a charity they get to be in charge of it.

A common experience of a non-profit start up is a group of like-minded individuals who reach a point where their part-time volunteering for a cause is not enough. They may need a place to meet, or a person to coordinate, or just the regular printing of information about their cause that cannot be done ad hoc. They realize their energy and dedication needs structure so they create a non-profit business.

This step can be a hard one, because they realize that much of the fun of the free spirited group camaraderie will be lost when a structure is imposed. The people who start charities are often different in their approach to starting, than people who start regular businesses. Mostly, people starting regular businesses planned to start the business. People who start non-profit businesses often had no intention of starting a business; they just wanted to help with a problem. The step from helper to entrepreneur may not be an easy or comfortable one.

There are, of course, people who plan from the start to create a new charity. They have a cause, and they want to set up an entity to help. Often they approach setting up a business as if it were just a larger version of their childhood lemonade stand. The danger is that a non-profit business is a business, not a hobby.

As I have mentioned, for any group, eager or reluctant to go into business, the 501 (c)(3) is often a splash of cold water in the face. It requires a great deal of paperwork. The government is not going to let anyone out of paying taxes until it is sure there is a real justification. The 501 (c)(3) is proof to a potential donor that someone has met the basic requirements to call themselves a charity. Without it, someone who gives the charity money may not be able to take a tax deduction for the gift. Anyone who tells people they are a tax-exempt charity without having that 501 (c)(3) can expect to be receiving help from those charities that do prison ministries.

All of these organizational issues are important, because it relates back to the issue of "good works" verses "good work".

People start charities to do good works, to help a cause. However, donors will give only if the charity does good work, as well as good works. Donors want to be sure that the new charity will use their money wisely and well in its efforts for the cause. They want the leadership of the charity to have their heart in the right place but donors also want the leadership's heads firmly on their shoulders. Being a non-profit business does not mean being a badly run business, a financially irresponsible business, or ultimately, a bankrupt business.

Running a non-profit business is hard work. It requires careful planning and reasonably certain financial support. Most new businesses fail, and that includes new charities. It is nothing to be ashamed of, because it is so easy to fail. Just remember, if you or others you know are thinking of starting a charity, that the mortality rate is very high. It isn't all that easy to be a "rock and roll star".

Chapter 35 Work

"Man's biggest mistake is to believe that he's working for someone else."
Nashua Cavalier (writer)

Do you ever get tired of your job? Do you ever feel envious of people who seem to have more interesting, better paying and more fun jobs? Well then, you are what is known in economic, medical, and theological circles as "normal". Almost everyone has some aspect of their work they are dissatisfied with. Most people at some time or another feel completely negative about their job. Some hate every single day of work.

I recently had a group of young volunteers come to help landscape at the agency. The day was hot, the ground hard, and the stones plentiful and large. After a few hours the teens were worn out. They still loved the Lord, and still wanted to help the poor, but they did not love that patch of ground. They did not even have the satisfaction of completion, because this project was going to take all summer, and there was still plenty of ground to turn. They had agreed to work, and hot, hard work is exactly what they got. No one can fault them for being happy to put those shovels down.

In charity work, both volunteers and staff can get burned out. Often regular volunteers suffer tremendous guilt when they finally stop helping. They know they could continue. They see others still working hard for the cause and know that the need still exists. Their fellow volunteers often consciously or unconsciously add to their guilt by trying to get them to stay. Church groups are notorious for having no term limits on projects or committees. You join and you are on for life. All too often, volunteers not only resign from a project but also withdraw from the church or charity completely. One reason is that they just cannot bear to face the other volunteers. I remember encountering a lady who had once been very active at my church. After a few minutes visiting and exchanging news of mutual friends I mentioned that it had been a long time since I had seen her. Her smile disappeared and she literally hung down her head. "I ran away," she said. "I was so busy and I did not want to hurt anyone's feelings by refusing to help but I needed a break." She had joined another church where she kept her volunteer activities to a minimum. I congratulated her on making a reasonable decision to regain control of her life. "I would love to go back just to say hello to people but I would feel so guilty. Do you think it would be OK?" she asked. I assured her everyone would be happy to see her and she had nothing to feel guilty about. I have not seen her since and I wonder if she has overcome her guilt feelings enough to feel comfortable visiting her old friends from the church.

A former volunteer feeling like a deserter is unfair and poor manpower utilization. Charities would be wise to provide a celebration when volunteers are ready to quit, a hail and farewell party that honors the work done, rather than begs for more. Volunteers are not stupid. They know that any thanks they receive during their volunteer service has an unspoken motivation of keeping them on the job. Thanks given when they quit is the only time that the charity's gratitude can be clearly perceived as free of any secondary motive. True gratitude from a charity is important for the charity to keep itself spiritually centered. A charity that feels ingratitude toward its helpers can become callus about its clients and the spirit of charity will vanish. After all, these volunteers have given the charity some service. The vast majority of citizens give a particular charity nothing.

Sadly, the staff and boards of charities can sometimes get their noses up in the air and decide that the "cause" is so noble that everyone has a duty to it. This is not so. In this world you have a duty to your country that is spelled out in the law. Service to any particular 501(c)(3) is not listed in scripture as necessary for salvation.

When we get a volunteer who has helped for two weeks, or six months, or four years we need to be happy and grateful. Charities that are humbly grateful for all the help they receive are much wiser institutions. They recognize that they have received free labor when they needed it.

There is an aspect of burnout that the volunteers need to understand. They have been working. They have not been playing or relaxing but working. Work is sometimes physically exhausting, emotionally frustrating, and psychologically damaging. The old saying that "hard work never killed anybody" is completely false. It kills lots of people. Several medical studies have documented the fact that there is a huge increase in heart attacks at 9:00 on Monday mornings compared to any other time and day of the week. This fact clearly contradicts the old "hard work ..." saying. When your body, mind, and spirit tell you it is time to quit then it is time to quit.

After all, as Cavalier said at the start of the chapter, we all work for ourselves. Volunteer work is work, not play, but we do it for ourselves, not for a boss. Most work is done for pay. With this pay we are able to buy ourselves the things we need to live. If we do not receive this pay we will not do the work. Volunteer's pay is of a different sort (gratitude, accomplishment and other feelings of spiritual satisfaction and joy), but it is still necessary for a full life. However, the needs of life change as we grow and change. Different work and causes may feed us better at a different time.

There is no good or bad in this need to change direction. Mother Teresa probably never raised money for the Salvation Army and Billy Graham has probably not been a major donor to the United Jewish Appeal. However, that has not stopped those two people from doing good work or those two causes from helping people. The cause was just not a match for the person at the time. If you stop volunteering for a particular cause, it does not mean you become a selfish worldly materialist. It is just a reshuffling of needs and priorities. Do not worry. There is another yoke out there somewhere that will fit just fine.

Chapter 36 Disaster and the Internet

"Three things it is best to avoid: a strange dog, a flood, and a man who thinks he is wise."
Welsh saying

Everything in the non-profit world seems to happen later than it does in the for-profit world and the use of computers was no different. Yet, the Internet has finally become a part of fundraising and shows signs of having the same long-term impact as in regular business. It is still too soon to see how all the possible changes Internet giving will affect non-profits and enough people are writing prediction articles and books without my adding to the crystal ball gazing. But one major aspect of giving that has gone through a major metamorphosis is the Internet response to major disasters.

In the last few years, three major disasters have played a major role in how Americans respond to disaster. The first was 9/11 and the destruction of the World Trade Center. For the computer generation, 9/11 was their defining moment.

Just as their parents remember where they were when President Kennedy was shot and their grandparents remember the moment they heard about Pearl Harbor, the youth of America were permanently imprinted by 9/11. It was an event that altered America at its core. The self confidence the country had enjoyed since the collapse of the Soviet Union ended, while simultaneously a unity of concern for fellow countrymen and a pride in the example of sacrifice shown by the police and firemen who died helping others emerged. Local and regional differences were put aside and people clearly identified themselves as Americans. One small indicator of this new unity was that while the sale of American flags rocketed upward the sale of Confederate flags dramatically dropped.

While television brought the images of disaster to Americans, the Internet played a large role in how people responded. First the phone systems overloaded and people could not call the relief agencies to offer help. Secondly, people found they could get more information on the Internet about how they could help than they could from television. Television only gave highlights and people wanted more data. Finally, as a result of complaints about how some of the organizations had handled aid distribution, people increasingly used the Internet to quickly evaluate various charities and decide where to send appropriate help. Donors discovered they could also learn which charities received negative reviews on their performance in order to avoid them.

Much of this negative knowledge came after the fact and 9/11 saw a high degree of anger and frustration about what to do and how. Donating via Internet was brand new and had never been used in such volume before. Even the news media seemed to be aware that their traditional role of reporting disasters needed to be revised. Reporting on a disaster and later reporting on people being dissatisfied with how certain charities responded was not enough. When the next big disaster hit the news media seemed to know it needed to report more than what had happened. Now, more than ever, people wanted to immediately know what kind of help was needed and where to send it. Because of the lessons Americans learned after 9/11 many would know how to use the Internet much more effectively when a disaster struck. It was a good thing because the next disaster was of mind-boggling size and horror.

On December 26, 2004, a tsunami killed, wounded, or impoverished hundreds of thousands of people in South Asia. People all over the world were stunned to learn whole communities were wiped out in a few minutes. This disaster created a worldwide response that began only minutes after the scope of the destruction was realized. This time the Internet played and even more important role. Charities all over the world recognized they needed to put their involvement and their needs on the Internet at once to allow the world to find an immediate way to help and to gain information. One reason this was very important was that the news media could not effectively report on what was happening because there was no way to get news crews into areas hit by the flood waters any sooner than the rescue teams themselves could get in. News teams in the path of the tsunami had met the same fate as everyone else.

Americans responded splendidly to the needs of the people around the Indian Ocean and showed that they had become much more sophisticated in the use of the Internet as a tool to aid in helping in an appropriate manner. I remember talking to a number of people with different religious and civic groups. In every case the people were deciding how best they could help through information they were searching out on the Internet. By the time of the third great disaster, America seemed ready to use the Internet to its full capacity and the test came only a few months later.

On August 29, 2005 Hurricane Katrina came ashore on the gulf coast. The devastation caused by the storm and the flooding of New Orleans is probably the greatest natural disaster to hit the United States since the 1906 San Francisco earthquake and fire. Americans responded with great generosity and the American charitable institutions rose to the occasion in a way that brought them much more love and respect than most of the governmental agencies especially FEMA.

By the time of Katrina, Internet giving had become a major factor in how Americans responded to disaster. Charities involved in relief work posted their needs and recommendations on how to respond on their web sites quickly. The news media sites also linked to these charity sites so that people seeking news would immediately know how to help most effectively. Another interesting feature of the maturity of Internet disaster giving was the number of blogs that showed up to evaluate how the charities were doing and to help the ones doing a good job. Blogs are all over the Internet these days and many serve as alternative information sources to the regular news media. Many people have gotten used to checking the opinions and viewpoints being expressed on these sites and they serve as a sounding board for popular issues.

The blogs reflected a positive view of how the mainstream charities were responding to the disaster and people saw how they might direct the type of help they wanted to give to do the most good. There were also plenty of warnings about scam charities that might put up web sites just as a way of getting money. When a major charity was seen as not doing a good job it was quick to draw criticism. (While not a charity, FEMA the Federal Emergency Management Agency received such loud criticism the director was forced to resign.) All in all, the Internet gave the country an electronic version of a combination gossip fence and town meeting to help move the right stuff to the right people in the right manner.

In many ways Katrina allowed more people to help in more ways than 9/11 or the tsunami. In 9/11 a large portion of the people were killed, and were thus beyond human help. With the Tsunami there was again a high death toll and great distance to send help. In both cases money was about the only effective help most people could offer. With Katrina, food, water, clothing, medical services, volunteer help and much more could be used if brought to the right place in the right manner. The Internet also made it possible to get information about loved ones cut off from phones and other communication devices. I remember my stepmother being frantic about her brother in New Orleans. She got her grandson to get on the Internet and use the satellite picture system to look at the house he lived in and make sure it was intact. She felt much better once she could see the house had not been damaged. Many people were able to determine the extent of damage to homes and property of friends and relatives with that system. Such things would have been impossible just a few years before.

The Internet may or may not replace mass mail for charities' general fund-raising but it has built for itself an important place in the work of effective charitable disaster relief. The importance of this cannot be underestimated because in an emergency a speedy and an effective response are generally the same. When people are injured, sick, starving or exposed to dangerous conditions waiting often equals being too late. The importance of the Internet in the charitable world may well be beyond the imagination of anyone.

Chapter 37 Donor Cultivation

"The diligent farmer plants trees, of which he himself will never see the fruit."
Tusculanarum Disputationum (I, 14)
Marcus Tullius Cicero (Roman statesman)

It is interesting and appropriate to use the language and imagery of the garden when discussing donors. This does not mean that donors are mindless passive vegetables. To get a great harvest of heads of lettuce from inside the heads of men, one must go to congress, or at least, the state legislature.

Such terms as planting, harvesting, and above all, cultivation are useful is they capture the image of time, effort, patience and diversity of circumstances that is so much a part of the donation process.

If you are in a hurry, then farming is not for you. Farming is the ultimate hurry up and wait game. Seeds need to be planted at exactly the right time and later, when the crop is ready, delaying harvesting will spoil the crop. However, in between those two critical busy periods is a long stretch of patient waiting, accompanied by regular maintenance and weeding. During this period you are at the mercy of nature. Too little rain, too much rain, sudden frosts, hail, insects, disease and even sunshine can ruin the crop. As a boy in Arkansas, I learned that you never asked for a prediction on the cotton crop. Only a fool made predictions about crops. One did what was reasonable and prudent and left the rest to the Lord.

There are also the variations between plants. Some want hot weather and some want cool. Some want wet and some want dry. Often their needs change as they grow. The hot weather necessary to crack open the cotton boles to expose and dry the cotton at the end of the season, will scorch and kill the same cotton plants earlier in the season. Even in the dormant season some plants will not survive a particularly cold winter, while others need the hard freeze to help them rejuvenate. Each year is different, each plant is different, and each patch of ground is different. As a boy I watched my grandfather stand in a huge field carefully discussing the relatively poor performance of a patch of ground you could cover with a bed sheet. Such terms as drainage and elevation meant nothing to me at that age. But those men knew. They were planning exactly how they would reshape and build up that patch of earth next winter, to increase the yield.

Donors are individuals. There is no way the agency beggar can have a formula to cover each donor in every situation. He can do what is reasonable and prudent and then he must wait for the donors to respond. The beggar has no control over how their overall financial situation is doing. He may face an enormous challenge overcoming their personal psychological attitude toward money. He cannot block out other pressures and demands on the donor's finances.

In the beginning, the beggar must move quickly to capture the interest and enthusiasm of a potential donor. The beggar is introduced to someone at a party, a mutual friend brings someone by to see the program, someone stops to ask a few questions after hearing a talk the beggar gives to a group or perhaps he gets a response to a mass mailing. The beggar must be ready with information, opportunities, and appreciation for that prospect's interest. Where, and at what pace, the relationship develops depends on an infinite number of variables. The beggar can only control a small percentage of those variables, and may never know many of them.

Prudence and patience are the best virtues for cultivation. Remember routine weeding and watering, but not the same routine for everyone. One cannot expect the same number of visits or donations from everyone, any more that one can grow cotton and cranberries together. The quality of the Development Department's information gathering and tracking is vital. The donor's history, interests and concerns need to be recorded and regularly checked. A beggar does himself no favors if he asks about a man's wife when the files recorded her obituary eight months before.

Cultivation of donors sometimes takes decades. What the charity will receive will not be plucked, but freely given. It may even happen long after the beggar who started the process, has left the organization. The beggar's reward is to become personally involved with really wonderful people, who genuinely care about the charity and want to see it prosper. This process may take a long time but should not be dull. Beggars will get to help the charity and help the donor as well. If this is not a win win situation the beggar has failed in his duty. The beggar must look out for the interests of the charity. That is his employer and that commands his ultimate loyalty. At the same time, he is the contact point between the charity and the donor. If the beggar fails to respond to the donor's concerns and wishes or permits the charity to do so, then the donor will have a legitimate grievance and a negative impression of the charity which can adversely affect future gifts from the donor and the charity's reputation. Thus if it is not everyone's win it will be everyone's loss and the beggar will have failed the charity and the donor at the same time.

At one time a major university had been cultivating a wealthy graduate for a gift. The school was planning an expansion of their business school and wanted money for a new building. The development staff met with the man to ask for a gift but the businessman indicated he wanted to help the university's agriculture school with a gift to memorialize his father. The development people said that was fine and the man made a large contribution. In their determination to finish the business school expansion the school ignored the donor's request and put the money into the business school building fund. Realizing they were not following the donor's wishes the university administration decided to placate him by naming the new building after his father. The school decided to surprise the businessman with the naming at the opening ceremonies. When the businessman arrived he was shown the new part of the business school named after his father and told how grateful the school was for his help. The businessman was furious about what the school had done. He told them that his father had been a farmer all his life, loved farming and cared nothing about business. The man was so angry he severed all ties with his old alma mater and while he gave large sums of money to various educational institutions over the years he never gave his own university another dime. The development department had failed to insure the donor's wishes were honored and in the process cost the school millions in future gifts.

If you are the beggar, enjoy your work of cultivation. It is better than gardening in countless ways. However, you don't get to use the Burpee seed catalogue and that is unfortunate, because the Burpee seed catalogue is great fun.

Chapter 38 Un-Americanism

"A man's poverty before God is judged by the disposition of his heart, not by his coffers."
Augustine of Hippo (Christian writer and saint)

It is possible there is much of the Judeo-Christian religion that is Un-American. I am not talking about the worship of sex or the worship of money, which is so much a part of modern America. Political forces on the left and right spend plenty of time blasting each other over these issues. The left will point out that the right supports business and consumerism and worships the World. The right notes that while the left talks of freedom of choice and ending hypocrisy and Puritanism they wind up following the Flesh. Both sides preach endlessly about the "sins" of the other and never address their own sins so some theologians can argue they both help the Devil. But I don't want to talk about the World, the Flesh and the Devil. In any case this book is about begging not politics.

What I want to discuss here is that for people who love God and country some of the great virtues that make America; America can present them with a dilemma. We Americans value self-reliance, rugged individualism, independence, freedom of thought, human dignity and above all democracy. Do not get me wrong, I am not saying these are bad things or that the faithful cannot practice them. However, many people of faith understand that they are confronted with a different set of values from God. To be good citizens is something St. Paul recommended to the Christians under Rome, "All things are lawful, but not all things are profitable. All things are lawful, but not all things edify. (1 Corinthians. 10:23)." Let me explain the dilemma that the values I spoke of can create.

As a beggar I often need to explain the value of giving away money. This can be quite a trick. But people often understand that to use money to make things better for others, also often makes it better for themselves and those they love. To put it bluntly, a kid playing ball on one of our teams is not stealing your car. With Christian groups I will often use this argument, but it has some problems. God says over and over to help people in need. Jesus Christ at the Last Supper gives a wonderful promise to those who do good to "the least of these" (Matthew 25:31-46) and a terrible prophecy of the fate of those who fail to act. However, what is never said is that we will end poverty by giving. There is never any guarantee that our efforts will produce results. In fact, there are several statements in the Bible that indicate mankind may never solve the problem.

This lack of success runs counter to much that we hold dear in America. We believe we can solve anything. We also believe in "God helps those who help themselves". Yet this is not the view of much of Christianity. Christians are to help those who cannot or will not help themselves. They are to help even if nothing is accomplished. They are to help because they are to act like Christ himself. We do this in very imperfect ways but we are supposed to do it. Christians know that if Christ only gives to people, if he is assured of seeing good results, in a timely manner, than he would not be the living example of the perfect love of God. Christians want to receive that perfect love so they are to try and reflect it into the world. The ancient Greeks believed the Gods sometimes rewarded heroes and the Norse viewed Valhalla as a place for heroes. A basic concept of Christianity is that heaven is for people who do not deserve it. Since Christians cannot reach perfection themselves how can they expect perfection from others? The self made man is a myth in the Christian world.

A response to this dilemma is that the American virtues are goals Christians want for others, but not for themselves. American Christians knows the strength and value of rugged individualism but recognize they are part of the body of Christ and are interdependent on each other like cells in a human body. They want people to be free, but they have a personal duty to God. They do not want to see other people made to feel ashamed, but they themselves reject the need for personal pride. All men are equal but Christians are servants of God and servants to mankind. Democracy is the most favored form of government, but the faithful also swear allegiance to a heavenly king.

When I am asking for money it is not a time for personal pride. Personally I am all too fond of pride. Yet I find the role of fool works better in fundraising. It is a role God understands completely. After all, God made us to sing and to fart. God ordained bird song to fall on our ears and bird poop to fall on our heads. God likes mud and maggots as much as flowers and fireflies. I have learned that folly is normal and unavoidable. So you have a choice, you can be a fool for Christ or a damned fool. But a fool you will be one way or another. And the biggest dammed fools of all are those concerned with their own dignity.

From my perspective I can ask for grants from foundations to meet all the American virtues. We will do something bright and new and solve a problem with their money such as ending poverty, enlightening the ignorant, providing social justice, and other good stuff. The faithful will just have to keep paying the bills to keep the doors open and volunteering to do the unglamorous work of helping people in need.

Chapter 39 Frustration

"Enjoy life. There's plenty of time to be dead."

Hans Christian Andersen (Danish writer)

Many in development suffer from frustration which seems reasonable enough. There is so much suffering and need, and the response of the world is so slow and pathetically inadequate. Development people are at particular risk because we are the part of a charity that supplies resources. Others are on the front line of the fight. The social worker, the doctor, the missionary, the public defender, the clergy and others are directly involved with the needy. They see the suffering, the illness, the fear, the pain and the death. Beggars are not on the front line. Beggars are just the supply depots.

The challenge is that we generally do not have all the supplies needed. Supplies in the non-profit world can be money, volunteers, donated goods, or donated services. While money is best because we can buy the other things, we find volunteers cut back on manpower expenses and it is sometimes easier to get food, medicine, office supplies, used clothes and other items from people or businesses than to get money to buy them. Food is an excellent example of a needed supply. At Thanksgiving and Christmas people donate food and clothing. Unfortunately, people need to eat all year long and come summer we are often short or have the wrong kind of food. Old Easter candy (donated candy generally shows up in the agency about three months after the holiday it was designed for) is not a substitute for baby food. Sometimes we have no food at all which can cause us great guilt. We beggars can find ourselves thinking that if we had done more or pushed harder we would have raised more money to help more. That sense of shame can make us lash out at the people who are doing the most and by that I mean the donors. We can blame them for not doing more when in reality we are angry and ashamed of ourselves for not doing more. This is a trap that must be avoided at all costs. Worry and guilt raise no money. The simple truth is that shortages are a normal aspect of charitable work.

It is ironic that we often get angry at the donors sooner than at the non-donors. I think it is because we know and care about the donors. They reflect our own interest in the cause, whatever it may be. Make no mistake about it; you will not survive in development if you have no interest in the cause you serve. The hours are too long, the work too demanding and the pay too low to keep you if you don't care. We have no relationship with the non-donors. We may respect them if they support other causes or we find them puzzling creatures if they care for nothing more than themselves. In many ways they can seem an abstract issue rather than real people. To understand this mindset one can turn to the words of John Wayne as he played Davy Crockett in his film,"The Alamo". He said; "There's right and there's wrong. Ya do the one and you're living. Ya do the other, and you may be walking around, but you're as dead as a beaver hat."

People with that mindset will get frustrated over their inability to help others. But I have to remember that my frustration is my problem not the world's. Frustration is the result of my trying to play God and get the cosmos to suit me. The real God knows I am not up to the task. Frustration is an appropriate punishment for the sin of pride. So if I take the fall after the pride that is my doing, not the world's. For a frustrated fundraiser remembering that he can always surrender his desire for control over to God can relieve the frustration. Once that happens the fundraiser accepts that his timetable may not be God's timetable and the fundraiser can let God set the schedule. Let me give you an example of God's time.

God's time is not our time. After all, God is eternal but we can only touch Him in the present. The past and the future are illusions that only exist in our minds. God uses time as He wants. He invented it and he can play with it if he chooses. Lately some physicists and writers have found quantum mechanics and other aspects of modern physics tend to tear linear time concepts apart. These discoveries reinforce the idea that the fullness of time may not be what we think.

One aspect of God acting in his own time I came across a few years ago. For around 2000 years Christians have been talking about being washed in the blood of the Lamb. There are any number of hymns saying how the blood will wash us clean. Obviously, if you wash yourself or your clothes in blood you do not get clean. You get sticky, red, and soon smelly. But for 2000 years people accepted this image when it made no sense. Now comes the modern world and modern medicine. We discover that inside us living blood does just what the Bible said. Not spilled dead blood on the alter but alive in us blood cleans as well as feeds. It meticulously washes away every impurity and dead cell in our body. Just so the blood of Christ is alive to wash the body of the church (that's us) as we live in Christ.*

Here is God having generation after generation recite this blood imagery and now, hundreds of generations later, He lets us in on his little biology secret. That it is not a metaphor or an analogy but a literal fact. If God felt man did not need an explanation of this image for almost 2000 years is may be that He will delay solving a financial problem for a local charity a bit longer than the average beggar is comfortable with. If we are willing to wait on His timetable we may be awestruck by the solution.

*Dr. Philip Brand and James Yancy wrote two books on the human body and various spiritual analogies that can be drawn from it. One is "In his Image" and the other is "Fearfully and Wonderfully Made". They are both great works and have deep insights that I draw from here.

Chapter 40 Santa

"Nothing that you have not given away will ever be really yours."
C. S. Lewis (English writer)

December is very important in the charity world as there is a great deal of giving then. Some people wait till the end of the tax year to make their gifts. These people are generous but understand that they get the same tax deduction on a gift at the end of the year as at the beginning. Investing the money until December has a strong appeal to people who plan their finances. However, there are other reasons December plays an important role in the world of charity.

For the last hundred years or so three traditional Christian holidays and one traditional Jewish holiday have drifted together in the minds of many Americans to make December the season of giving. Hanukkah, the Festival of Lights marks the purification of the Temple of Jerusalem in 165 BC. Christmas celebrates Jesus' birth and Epiphany commemorates his adoration by the Magi and their presentation of gifts. On December 6th the church remembers Nicholas the Bishop of Myra who tradition says secretly gave some gold as a dowry for three poor girls so they might marry. It is from this man that we get the tradition of Santa. These events plus years of advertising by the merchants of America has developed a culture that believes in giving gifts in December. Even people who have no interest in religion will buy presents for family and friends in December. There is a celebratory atmosphere in America from Thanksgiving to New Years that is generally referred to as the Holiday Season. Santa takes center stage during this time and his image can be seen everywhere.

There are countless criticisms of Santa from all directions. Parents are concerned about children being deceived concerning the existence of a man from the North Pole who sneaks into homes at night bringing gifts. They are worried about the emotional scarring the children receive when they find out Santa isn't real. Some church members feel the emphasis on buying gifts makes America too materialistic and detracts from the true religious meaning of the season. Psychiatrists point out that the Holiday Season is hard on those whose lives are not as happy as the sentimental images offered in the media and that the suicide rate goes up during the Holidays. Police see increased family fights, drunk drivers and other results of people becoming stressed by the Holidays. Santa has some serious critics.

Yet, with all the Hollywood hype, the Madison Avenue commercializing and the legitimate complaints of the critics, Santa is an icon the charitable world has reason to admire and love. He comes with gifts. Every child understands that these are gifts, not loans, mutual obligations, nor merchandising ploys but pure gifts. Even more wonderfully they are appropriate gifts. Tradition says that Santa knows what children want and picks the right gift every time.

In the great American Santa mythos, Santa never makes a mistake. His toys are individually made with love and skill to match the hopes and dreams of each child. And most glorious of all is the abundance. Santa is lavish. He does not skimp. As a child, I remember debating with my friends about the existence of Santa. My strongest argument was that I knew my parents loved me but they did not have the money for the wonderful gifts I received each year. My friends tended to agree with me on this point because we had all had the experience of asking our moms to buy us things when we were in the stores and hearing them say "no, it costs too much, maybe you should ask Santa." Santa always seemed to hear and the item would appear Christmas morning.

In the world of charity, donors like Santa would be the answers to prayers. Donors who would give exactly what was needed when it was needed and give in such abundance that the charities could not only provide for the needs of the moment but begin to address those needs the charities never dreamed they would have the resources to tackle. Beggars love and respect their donors, and every little bit helps, but sometimes one cannot help but dream of the huge gift that will lift the charity up to a different level of service.

This is the sort of donor we each wish we were. We wish we were Santa. We wish we had the knowledge to do what is appropriate and the wealth to give with exuberance. We all wish we could just show up, help people and ride off amid the cheers to help someone else. That is why we, as a society, still want to believe in Santa. We know enough about ourselves to suspect we would not have the strength of character to maintain our personalities as Santa. Greed, pride, fear, sloth and countless other aspects of our personality would stop us. Yet we do not want to let go of that part of ourselves that loves and wants to help. Santa, the exuberantly generous giver touches us in a very profound way.

Chapter 41 Testimonials

"Tell me and I forget. Teach me and I remember. Involve me and I learn."

Benjamin Franklin (statesman and inventor)

When one is trying to raise money for a charity it is reasonable to try and utilize every resource possible. While the Development Department is the part of a charity responsible for the fundraising, to what degree can that department utilize the manpower of the charity's other departments? If there are recipients of the charity's help such as students, patients, the disabled, the poor or whatever group the charity serves, can they be involved in raising the money? While it is generally understood that Board members, the agency director, volunteers and even donors can be used to help fundraise, the use of other staff and or clients is a more unclear area with both benefits and problems. Charities must look at issues of manpower utilization, ethics, privacy and morale in deciding when or if to use staff or clients to help beg. This is an issue people need to be aware of even if they are not involved with a charity. It can have a direct bearing on how a charity relates to the public at any time.

A basic problem with using non development staff to fundraise is it takes them away from their real job. A school's teachers, hospital's doctors, museum's curators or homeless shelter's social workers cannot help the people their charity exists to help if they are out begging. The donors will be concerned about the fact that no work is being done. There is also a question about how effective such people will be outside the job they were hired and trained for. Many charities feel the staff is doing the work that is the reason for the charity's existence and they should be left alone to do it.

I can testify to the fact that donors and volunteers respond more favorably to program staff as spokespersons, than development staff in the same role. People prefer to hear from the people directly involved in the work. I was fortunate to have some people at my agency that were wonderful speakers. The man who ran our job placement program was a respected expert on the issues of jobs and poverty. He was often sought out by the local news media when a story related to those areas needed expert information. He was passionate, knowledgeable and articulate and enjoyed the respect of the news media and many area politicians. I was delighted that he was happy to attend our donor functions. Whatever table he sat at the donors at that table came away impressed with the great work we were doing in helping people get jobs.

The director of our Day Care had church groups that regularly wanted to hear her speak about the Day Care. She was also delighted to help out at our special events and over the years had become close friends with many of the major donors. I was particularly fortunate because the list of program staff that were willing, happy and able to speak for the agency was a long one. The director of our programs for seniors, our youth program director, the head of our drop in Day Care, our social workers and a number of other staff could and did relate their personal experiences to various individuals and groups over the years. Time after time donors increased their support after hearing from the people working on the front lines.

On one occasion the Executive Director's assistant and the agency's bookkeeper were at a large dinner for area charities. One of the other people at the table asked them where they worked. They began to tell about the agency and its history. It turned out that the man they were talking to was with the local public television affiliate. He was so impressed with the story that he persuaded the station to feature the agency in a film segment on a show about the city. A ten minute TV special was the result of these two employee's testimonial about where they worked. The Executive Director and I discussed the whole thing afterward and agreed that if we had been there instead of those two employees we would not have captured the attention of the people at the table the way they did.

A charity does not want to overwork or over burden the staff. In most charities the staff is busy just doing their jobs. Like all people everywhere staff may be uncomfortable speaking to strangers especially in large groups. If a charity wants to use the staff to fundraise it needs to do so with prudence. At the same time staff can bring a degree of expertise, personal experience and passion into their contacts with donors and donor prospects that cannot be found elsewhere.

I owe a deep personal gratitude to the staff where I worked because they were very willing to help when they could and I know they motivated many donors. Thus as in many things, there are two sides to this issue and the public needs to understand there are variables that cause one charity to present itself to the world differently than another.

The other major group that a charity might consider using to help raise money are those who directly benefit from the charity. At one end of the spectrum a famous alumni of a school using his name to help promote the school is widely accepted as a terrific asset and few schools are unwilling to utilize such an asset. The alumni, often understands the value of the education he received and is happy to help. At the same time, a former drug addict may be grateful to the drug rehabilitation program that helped him but find the memory of that dark period in his past so painful that he wants to avoid involvement in any activity that will remind him. Unlike the school alumni, such a person might also be reluctant to have his past generally known in the community.

I have had the honor of hearing some people give wonderful testimonials about getting their lives on course as a result of their coming to my agency. To actually meet and hear from someone who has benefited from the charity a donor supports makes the charity's work more real to that donor. Yet, I have always moved with great caution in this area. The executive Director had always insisted that no client feel any pressure to indorse the agency just because they received help there. As he put it, "no one needs to sing for their supper around here." I worked closely with the program staff and if there was some type of event coming up where some sort of client speaker would be beneficial I left it up to them to contact a person they felt would be comfortable in the role. We never considered any current client going through a crisis but rather someone who could tell of their past challenges and triumphs. We had a number of people that were happy to talk about how their lives had been changed for the better.

The one area where we would use people involved with the agency directly were kids in our youth program. Our youth director would often have youth finishing high school and were happy to speak about growing up in our youth program. They were often shy and nervous but they spoke will strong conviction about the fun they had, their plans for collage and how much they would miss the agency and all their friends. As I mentioned before this was only done with kids the youth director knew were willing to participate and whose parents gave full approval. Our agency always had a number of area residents on the Board and maintained a high degree of transparency in the neighborhood so the families knew what the youth were doing. Often public speaking was part of the high school kids' class work and this put them in front of an audience of supportive and admiring adults. The youth director was one of our greatest assets and saw to it that if the youth helped in any fundraising project that they had a good time and also felt they had helped the agency. Most of them had to complete a certain amount of community service work for graduation and they were delighted to complete their hours by helping their favorite agency.

While I cannot over estimate the value of client involvement in fundraising I must state it is not appropriate for everyone.

We never used clients who might be uncomfortable about helping. We were very sensitive to the clients self respect and privacy. With many types of charity work using the clients is not possible. A shelter for battered women, a program for the mentally disturbed or an AIDS treatment facility may all have very compelling reasons why their clients cannot help fund raise or in some cases even have their photos shown on an agency flyer. If your favorite charity never has pictures of the people they are helping they may have a very good reason other than that no one knows how to use a camera.

Chapter 42 Bumper Stickers

"How can you expect a man who's warm to understand a man who's cold?"
One Day in the Life of Ivan Denisovich
Alexander Solzhenitsyn (Russian writer)

Within their limited resources the poor are very good givers. They often give a larger percentage of their income then people with more. The poor will not give much because they do not have much. But the poor will often give sacrificially. In other words, they will give enough to negatively impact their own daily lives. In my city the local newspaper has a large giving program in December. Other charities as well as ours submit stories of needy clients and the press asks the public to give gifts to meet the described needs. In one case a few years ago an elderly woman wanted to go visit a sick relative in another part of the country. The program raised $100 to get her a bus ticket for the trip. Then by pure coincidence a friend of hers needed to make a trip to the area and gave the lady a free ride there and back. She made the trip and still had the $100.

The media program said they did not want it back, so she could do, as she wanted. She donated the money to us. We were concerned. This woman was living on less that $6000 a year but the lady explained to our social worker that she had never had $100 to give and our agency had helped her and her friends so often she really wanted us to have the money. She was happy to give something in thanks.

I do not know all about Heaven or even all about this woman, but if my assignment for all eternity is to shine this woman's shoes I will have received a much greater honor than I deserve. This is the living example of the story of the Widow's Mite in the Bible. In Mark 13:41 Jesus was watching people put money into the temple treasury. Among the rich and important people making large donations was a widow who put in two small coins. Jesus pointed out to his disciples that the widow was the most generous because though her gift was small it was all the money she had. I have seen this kind of sacrificial giving often enough to know it is not unusual among those who have very little.

Several years ago there was a terrible flood in Bangladesh. One of the poorest countries in the world Bangladesh was unable to provide aid to the people trapped and homeless by the flood. Death from starvation, drowning and disease threatened millions of lives. Individuals and countries around the world sent help. One of the centers for coordinating the relief work was set up in Calcutta India because it was close to Bangladesh. The news of the disaster spread through the city of Calcutta from one end to the other. Soon after the news broke the relief workers were informed that a delegation from the Calcutta street beggars wished to see them. The street beggars of Calcutta wanted to know if they could help the relief effort. A Calcutta street beggar is about as poor as a person can get. They live from hand to mouth with no home and no security. Starvation is their constant companion. Yet these people volunteered to assemble what tiny resources they could muster to help the flood victims. It may be that poverty makes a person more sympathetic than others to misery. It may also by that poverty gives a person faith in something other than possessions. They can release what meager possessions they have because they know possessions are not the answer. I do not know why poor people can be as generous as they are, I can only testify to witnessing numerous examples of their generosity.

Another generous group is the wealthy. I know people who do not think the rich ever act in any other than a selfish, greedy manner. Yet recently the two richest men in America (Bill Gates and Warren Buffet) gave the largest donation in history. The rich do not give so much that they stop being rich but they give much. It is true that many rich people give nothing. It is also true that many poor and middle class people give nothing. Without the support of the rich who do give, most charity work would not happen. The rich have many motives for giving, such as altruism, gratitude or even peer pressure and they often want to have a say in how their money is used, or at least be assured that it is used effectively. (This is particularly true if they wish to have a major impact with their gift.) Their influence affects who gets the money, how it is used, and what progress and accountability feedback is required, but charity in America would be in terrible trouble without the gifts of the rich.

Most people want to help but greed can often block the generous impulse. These days Materialism seems to be the philosophy that encourages greed. I like amusing bumper stickers. Yet some bumper stickers seem to be popular justifications for greed and materialism. The most blatantly materialistic was popular a few years ago and said, "The one who dies with the most toys, wins." I always wanted to ask, "Wins what"?

But as I said, I like bumper stickers. One I saw recently said "I started out with nothing and I still have most of it". I can identify with that completely.

Chapter 43 Eating Dirt

"We do not exist for ourselves."

Thomas Merton (Trappist monk and author)

Let us examine a much maligned and much misunderstood virtue called humility. Humiliation that is forced on someone is a real evil. People will often say they would rather die than face severe humiliation. The image of being shamed, degraded, mocked, spat upon and made to eat dirt is an experience people want to avoid. Yet the person who strives to achieve personal humility does not fit that image at all. Humble people are not in the dirt eating business. If you meet someone who tells you how small and humble they are your experiences in such matters will often cause you to doubt their sincerity. Such people are all too often self-pitying or have "false" modesty. False modesty is sometimes a defense mechanism. I will say something bad about myself to block you from saying it. Children will often confess to a parent to block a sibling from telling on them. This is a technique designed to soften the blow. False modesty is also a way to get praise from others. "Oh, I don't deserve this!" "Oh, but you do!" "Oh, no you are too kind!" "Oh it is the least we can do!" This is also known as fishing for compliments.

This behavior trait is normal human nature. We want love, we need praise and encouragement, and we will often act modest to get an extra dose. It is sad that we as individuals seem so love starved and unappreciated that most of us will do this occasionally and some of us do it constantly. However, people can quickly tire of this behavior from others and it does not enhance one person's respect for another.

This false behavior has nothing to do with true humility. The two become confused because the realistic appraisal of talents and abilities given by the humble person may sound momentarily like self-pity or false modesty. Any time spent with a truly humble person will show the difference but humble people are somewhat rare and many people may never meet the genuine article. In case you have not I will give you a little more information.

Almost everyone who has met a truly humble person likes them. People like them a lot. For one, they take a real interest in others. They will listen when you talk and respond in an open and honest way. They are helpful and patient and interesting to be around. They will talk about their ideas and interests but not overly about themselves. They want to hear about you. They are great listeners. They are also honest and fair.

The reason for this honesty is at the core of humility. The humble man has made the separation between self and value. He can appreciate something at the same level of quality if it is his or someone else's. His work is no better or worse for being his than someone else's. Thus the humble man is like the medieval Christian Saint, Francis of Assisi. The sun is his brother and the moon his sister. He takes no more pride in himself than in the dirt at his feet. He is going to be as interested in you as in himself.

When I decided to change careers in my early forties it was not easy. I was in a new city with few friends or contacts and none in the field of development. I would follow up on job leads and see anyone who might help me. I had a talk with a Catholic priest at a local high school who gave me the name of another priest at the Catholic university who might have some ideas. I am not a Roman Catholic and being new to the city and ignorant I did not realize I was trying to set up a meeting with one of the most important men in the area. He was a legend in fundraising that could get million dollar donations for the university with a phone call. His work over the years was a major factor in the considerable growth in size and prestige of the university.

I had asked for a twenty minute meeting but when I arrived at nine he spent the rest of the morning with me. He discussed my career plans in depth, gave me a list of people to contact and went out of his way to be helpful. I was a stranger he had no obligation to help yet he took a real interest in my situation and showed a genuine concern about helping me. Not long after I found the job I wanted and sent him a note to let him know and to thank him for the time and help he had given me. Over the years I occasionally ran into him at a professional fundraising association gathering. He always asked about my work and what I was doing. I obtained some first rate advice from him over the years and he was always generous with his time and knowledge. At one point years later he asked me to contribute a short written work to a national seminar he was giving. I was both honored and delighted to have a chance to show my appreciation for everything he had been happy to do for me over the years.

I tell this story not because I was someone special to him but because I was not. Everyone I encountered in the fundraising world who knew him had such stories. He took a keen interest in the charitable community as a whole and helped numerous professionals with the same degree of interest and concern he showed me. There was never any hint of his being too important or too busy for others. Still I know he was very important to the university and very busy as well. He served his church and his university to the best of his ability until his death. It was a great honor to know him.

Such a person feels connected to everyone. He can be a very effective fund-raiser because he can ask money from a stranger in the street with the same calm assurance of a child asking a goodnight kiss from a loving parent. Every man is his father; every woman is his sister, every insect on the ground, his child.

As I said it is easy to get misled about humility because the truly humble are rare. Humble people happen to show up in the world of charity more often than other places and it is a treat when they do. I do not want to confuse humble with weak. Moses who defeated the power of Pharaoh, lead the children of Israel for 40 years, and spoke to God face to face was described as humble. There are truly humble people out there. In working for charity I have met one or two humble people and the memory is an undying place of wonder.

Chapter 44 Showing the Flag

[30.38] Then give to the near of kin his due, and to the needy and the wayfarer; this is best for those who desire Allah's pleasure, and these it is who are successful.

[30.39] And whatever you lay out as usury, so that it may increase in the property of men, it shall not increase with Allah; and whatever you give in charity, desiring Allah's pleasure-- it is these (persons) that shall get manifold.

The Koran (Chapter 30 The Romans)

At one time or another, most charities will have a chance to display their programs to the public. It is not all that uncommon to go to a shopping mall, a community craft fair, or the student union of the local college and see one or more tables with information about charities in the area. Even regular trade fairs, car shows and home shows may offer charities free booths if the people putting on the fair cannot sell enough spaces to the business they are trying to promote. The charity's volunteers or staff will be at the display to supply information about the charity and offer opportunities for the public to help. Local United Way programs, chambers of commerce and other civic groups sometimes sponsor charity trade fairs where people in the community can come and find out about all the ways they can volunteer or donate in the area.

Over the years I have helped staff dozens if not hundreds of these booths. Because my charity was church related we often set up the booth at mission fairs. A mission fair is a way for a church or synagogue to show the membership all the ways they can become more involved in everything from joining the choir, the quilting circle, casserole clubs, scout troops to volunteering with one of the churches outreach missions. Even if the members who wander through the fair do not join anything they still want to be reassured that their congregation is reaching out to people. Such displays, of numerous activities, tell the congregation that they are members of an active and involved community. Even the most loyal members of a congregation appreciate that reassurance.

With time, I have learned a few things about these displays. The first thing I learned was not to sit down because no matter how tired my feet got if I sat down I was certain to have someone walk up at that moment to ask a question. If someone makes the effort to walk over to my display I want to be on my feet so I can greet them at eye level, move around the display and show them things and make them feel welcome and valued. It helps me to remember that the stranger who comes up to my booth and listens to what I have to say may become a major supporter in the future. I remember one man was brought over to my booth by his friend. We talked for a little while and a few days later he came by the agency to see it for himself. A few months later he was serving on the Board of Directors.

A public display is a form of advertising and results may not always be easily measured. The display may serve no other purpose than "showing the flag", a reminder to the world that your agency is still around. Such displays warm the hearts of friends and supporters. My most frequent guests at any such displays were people who had been involved with my agency in the past. They might be volunteers, donors or former clients and staff. These people just wanted to drop by, wish us well and enquire about people from the old days. Once someone has become involved with a charity they may loose interest and drift away but they will always retain a warm spot in their heart for the charity. The tie may not be as strong as an alumnus has for their old school but it is still there. As a result much of the time at trade fairs is spent listening to people describe their past encounters with the charity. If the people staffing the booth know their business they will let these people reminisce as much as they want. Often these memories will rekindle an interest in the charity and a desire to help.

Another visitor the booth often gets are people in need of the services the charity offers. While most of these displays are designed to provide the charity with publicity for fund raising and volunteer recruitment, they can also be to inform the public of services in the community. Charities that fight diseases often have people coming by to get information because they or someone they know suffers from the disease and they want to see what options there are. Charities related to the arts get questions from artists and performers about job opportunities. Schools get questions about enrollment or scholarships and so on. None of this makes any money for the charity but it does allow the charity to help those in need and that is its reason for existence.

One Saturday afternoon I was staffing a booth at a church mission fair. The church had set up a community mission fair to let people in the area know what types of services were available. Attendance was poor and I was spending a lot of time just standing around. I was bored and annoyed because it was a beautiful Saturday afternoon outside and I was missing it. Most of my fellow workers at the other booths were getting that blank stare that goes with boredom. A couple came in and wandered over to my booth. They introduced themselves as from a new independent church getting started in the area. They were meeting in a local movie theater until they raised enough money to build their own church. I said I understood that what they were doing was a fairly common way for a church to operate in the early stages of its existence. I asked them why they had come to the fair and they explained they were completely unfamiliar with the concept and had just dropped in to see what it was all about. They wanted to know how such an event was organized and what did it cost to put one on. I explained that such events were not complicated but did require advance planning and advertising to bring the general public. I then mentioned that most such mission fairs were directed at the church's own congregation and that advertising was much less of a problem. They were surprised to hear that such a setup would be directed towards one's own congregation. They asked me if I would mind explaining the concept in more detail.

For the next hour I told them everything I could about the organization and value of a mission fair. They had lots of questions and I tried to give them as clear a picture as possible. I explained that most charities were happy for an opportunity to display information and they would often have a trained professional present to answer questions. If someone wanted to have a number of charities in a location at a certain time he just needed to write and ask. I recommended a six month minimum lead time from the first request for displays to the event itself. I pointed out the longer the fair lasted that the more difficult it was for charities to recruit people to staff it and three to four hours on a Sunday morning was fairly common as people could come by between the various services and gather information about ways to volunteer in the community. I mentioned that a large protestant denomination had done a study on why people join churches and had found newcomers consider it very important that the church be involved in outreach to the community. The people might not participate in the various outreach efforts but they did want to know the church was active in helping in the community.

The couple thanked me for my time and information, asked for my business card, left and I thought no more about it. It had been a slow time and I was happier talking to them than standing around. When the fair was over I packed up the display and went home. It had been a fairly normal mission fair.

Almost a year later I was surprised to receive a letter from the wife of the couple I had met. She informed me that their church had put on a mission fair and it had been a great success. She told me they had seen a spurt in growth as a result and an increase in activity from the membership. She was very grateful for my advice and wanted me to know they had put it to good use. She said everything was going very well and she expected the church to start its building program sooner than expected.

One can argue that my time spent with these people accomplished nothing for my charity. However such a narrow view misses the fact that these people had used my information to help motivate a group of people to become more active in the general welfare of the community. That many more people helping others open up the possibility they may help some of my charity's clients. Even if their efforts don't directly impact our clients they help make the world better for all of us. That is a good thing in itself and something my charity and all charities want to have happen. The more people helping the better!

Chapter 45 Charity

"It is more blessed to give than to receive."

The Bible; Acts, 20:35

In the non-profit world a charity is an organization that does good. However, the word charity literally means love. The three words St. Paul speaks of as being the most important are Faith, Hope and Charity (First Corinthians 8). But none of these are abstract or passive words. St. James says that faith without works is dead (James 2). After all to believe in God means nothing. Traditional Christians would argue that Satan believes in God as do all the devils in Hell. There may be atheists in foxholes but definitely there are none in Hell. The argument is that Satan believes in God, he just does not believe God. The world has many people in the same camp. They say they believe in God but clearly they don't believe

Him. They reject some, or all, of what the Bible states is the word of God. At some time or another, to one degree or another, we all seem to practice this kind of faith. We act as if God were lying, or joking, or miss-translated, or misunderstood. For many of us, the word allegory is used as a kind of spiritual whitewash to cover any aspect of God's word we don't want to face as truth.

I am aware that the Bible states God gave Ten Commandments to Moses. One of these says we are not to murder and I never have. I understand that murder is a very evil act and I have never done it. The same Ten Commandments include one about keeping the Sabbath day holy and not working. I have ignored this Commandment on a regular basis. I may have gone to church in the morning but I often spent the rest of the day in normal, worldly, pursuits including working. I have not found any statement in the Bible to show that some of the Commandments are serious and others mere suggestions. My point is that I am just as willing as the next person to ignore what God says and I see no evidence of my obedience improving.

Yet, I hope for improvement and for forgiveness. The dictionary shows that hope comes from the same root as hop or leap or dance. Here we see faith in action. A ballet dancer will throw herself across the stage into the arms of her partner. She has faith in her talent, and his, to make such a jump come out right. However, she is taking a chance that she, or he, will err, and she might sail into the orchestra pit. Her faith is strong enough to let her launch herself into the air where her only parachute is hope. Hope is the literal leap of faith.

Faith cannot be a matter of reason or evidence. To believe that dropping a bowling ball on your foot will hurt is not faith. That is experience and reason working together. You have plenty of experience with both gravity and pain to reason out that bowling ball, plus gravity, plus foot, equals pain. That is not faith, that is math.

In the movie "Indian Jones and the Last Crusade" Harrison Ford must take a leap of faith. He is standing at the edge of a chasm and must step off into it. As Jones, Harrison Ford is playing a man of science, who must put his faith in the work of another scientist (his father) and hope it will be all right.

Whether one has faith in science, religion, or both, people demonstrate faith in other people. The direct religious experience is very rare, and no one has the time or money to perform all the experiments for oneself that prove the various aspects of science. In both cases, the faithful trusts the honesty and accuracy of the providers of information. And in both cases, there is plenty of evidence to cause faith to falter and die. Let me give a few examples.

For Jews, even as far back as the Babylonian captivity, the story of the prophet Daniel catching priests faking the divine aspects of the god Bel was recorded in the Apocrypha. The churches of Europe display enough nails to fill a barrel, each supposed to be from Christ's crucifixion. Not to mention the forest of splinters from the "true cross" itself. God only knows how many varieties of trees these come from. At the same time, science has everything from Piltdam Man and Clever Clarence the mathematical horse, to Cold Fusion and Phrenology to show it can be led astray.

This list of corrupt clergy faking miracles and corrupt scientists faking data is longer that either group wants to admit. There are also the honest mistakes, covered up out of fear of embarrassment, and the mistakes never noticed. We only know about the ones that have been spotted and live with hope, that whatever our creed, the unfound errors will not destroy us. This testing is hard on any soul and we see side effects in the fanatical, angry stands taken by so many, who feel, but dare not admit, that their faith is breaking under the strain. These side effects can be horrible and dangerous, but are also sad and deserve our pity.

Now we come to charity. Faith without works is dead and charity is the most alive one can be. In charity one is no longer separate, but a living member of the whole. By member, I do not mean a cipher in the head count of a group, but a body part. A hand is not an eye, nor an ear a tongue, but each serves the body well, in a unique way, that is only possible in membership. A hand also serves itself, in a much more complete way, than it ever could on its own. A severed hand, in a jar, might be kept alive for a scientist to study muscle and nerve reactions, but it can never do much that matters. Attached to the proper body it can dress a wound, paint a picture, write a love letter or caress a child.

Charity is most definitely about the here and now. Love is not something you plan for the future or consider as a philosophic point. You fall in love. Faith is where you start, Hope is your action, and when you make your hopeful leap of faith you fall. Yes you fall in love. Don't worry; there is no bottom so you won't hit your head. Also you can't drown because it's living water. As a matter of fact you are only in danger of dying of thirst never of drowning. Once you hit the big pool you turn into water yourself, and no one who comes in contact with you will be in danger of dying of thirst, either. And the water will gush like a geyser out of you. Oddly, you will not see anything different about yourself. You will still have many of the same doubts and fears, the same tired feet, and the same itchy places. In the movie "The Wizard of Oz" Frank Morgan as the wizard tells the Tin Woodsman "A heart is measured not by how much you love, but by how much you are loved by others". It is through the action of Charity that we reveal how open our hearts are.

To love others we must love ourselves. This is easier said than done. If you were fortunate enough to have a happy childhood, with love and support all around, this loving may be second nature. However, self-respect and self-love may be difficult for many to hold, if they never experienced it as children. For them, charity may be an alien duty that they feel they must do rather then something they do naturally. Not to worry, love can become a learned habit, just like brushing your teeth. The smile when you feel like frowning, the kind word when you feel like growling, or the generous act when you feel like resting, are all habits you can learn. They will become second nature because they are natural. All love can become self-love, if you recognize your membership. After all, you are a reflection of everything else and everything else is a reflection of you. You are trading atoms with the cosmos, by the billion, every second, so to think of yourself as isolated is unnatural.

For Christians rejection of isolation is very important. They must find the face of Christ in every face. You do not have to like your brothers and sisters, but there is kinship, and you must hold them special, as members of the family. The words of Christ are to "love your neighbor as you love yourself". If one claims to love Christ one must love others. One can still become angry; after all, even happy siblings sometimes fight. That is not the issue. If one does not see the face of Christ in all God's other children, how will that person spot the family resemblance when they meet God? Will he not be alien? Charity begins at home, but for the Christian, home is everywhere and your closest relative is anyone on the planet. This may be a difficult issue, as you look over your relatives but remember: you pick your friends, God picks your kin.

Chapter 46 Funerals

"No one's death comes to pass without making some impression, and those close to the deceased inherit part of the liberated soul and become richer in their humanness."
Hermann Broch (Austrian writer)

A long time supporter of my charity just passed away. The visitation is tomorrow and I will go. I also go to a number of funeral services. I don't enjoy these events and yet I am happy to attend. The person who has died is someone I respect and honor. This is true in every case when I go to the funeral of a volunteer or donor. These are people who have done much, over the years, to help my agency and they deserve to be honored.

These donors are usually elderly and their deaths, like their lives, tend to follow a pattern. They have been active with the agency, well up into old age, and then something happens to them. Generally, they get sick or incapacitated in some way, and can no longer volunteer. Often they will ask to be removed from the donor list because they are in such poor health they have let some family member is take over their finances. We always do as they ask but continue to send them newsletters, so they can stay informed.

When they finally pass away, the family is always pleased to have someone from the agency attend the service. The family members tell me how much the agency meant to their mother, or grandmother, or sister, as the case may be. The departed donors or volunteers are more often women, and if they were married, they are now generally widows. This is just how the pattern plays out.

Something else almost always happens at these funerals. The family tells me how much their loved one cared about the agency. Even if we have not seen her in several years the family talks of how recently she spoke of us. I am always happy to tell them how much we valued their loved one and what a wonderful job she did. This is not hard, for I work for an old charity and these women have volunteer histories that go back 20, 40, even 60 years! In some cases, they have been helping others since before I was born.

Our agency had been started by the women of the church over a hundred years ago. While the agency had a regular Board of Directors the women of the church had maintained their own representative board that primarily functioned as a volunteer work pool and as a link back to the congregations they came from. One of the funerals I attended was for a long time member of this Women's Board. She had first become involved with the agency as a child coming down to help with her mother. When a sudden illness in her late eighties made it impossible for her to continue volunteering we all knew the end was near. She passed away not long after and her funeral was attended by both friends and family. When her family spoke of her they kept saying how much the agency had meant in her life. As was often the case at these events the family had requested that people make gifts to the agency in lieu of flowers. The family knew it was what she would have wanted.

When we get these memorial gifts we do not try and pursue the donors to see if they will continue giving. We understand that they are giving to honor the dearly departed rather than because they care about the work of the agency. Yet I find these memorlal gifts very touching. I remember the faces of the ladies they memorialize and I am awestruck by the depth of love and commitment these ladies have made. Even after death they have reached out and helped a little more for their beloved charity. A tangible proof that love is so powerful even death cannot block it.

Because I grew up in the South, attending funerals has been something I have done from a very early age. Many people consider it inappropriate or even harmful for children to go to funerals. However, I was raised to understand that when someone died you went to the funeral. As my grandparents grew more enfeebled and unable to attend the funerals of their elderly friends, I was sometimes sent as the "family representative" to the funerals of people I didn't even know! So I have been to a number of funerals.

Funerals can be a reflection of the effect the "dearly departed" has had on people. This may not always be a positive thing. But, my experience at funerals of people whose lives have been dedicated to helping others has been a worthwhile one. These affairs tend to be warm and gentle. Tears are common but despair and gloom are rare. Such people leave a positive legacy. I am always happy to do what I can to honor their memory.

Chapter 47 A Check List for Begging and Life

"It is always safe to learn, even from our enemies; seldom safe to venture to instruct, even our friends."
Charles Caleb Colton (English cleric and writer)

I am writing this last chapter to the professionals in the world of development. If you are not a professional beggar you are welcome to look over my shoulder and hear what I would to say to my peers. It can't hurt and you can go out into beggar-land with this little checklist and see if the profession is paying any attention.

Dear fellow beggar, if you are the sort of person that likes lists, rules, formulas and instructions then this chapter is just for you. There are some basic cookbook rules that can help the beggar avoid failure and many of them apply to life in general. So here is a basic rulebook that has served me well.

Plan ahead: With special events in particular and most fund raising in general scheduling a year or two in advance is essential. Your fund raising campaign cannot be hit or miss (your agency needs a projection for its overall budget) and you need to know in advance that in May you will have a gala dinner, in June a mass mailing, and in July a newsletter. Buying supplies, renting banquet halls, and scheduling staff and volunteer time needs to be laid out well ahead of the deadline. With a really big special event you have to start planning years in advance.

Be flexible: Your job is to raise money, not merely to put on special events or send out mailings. If something alters or blocks your plans - adjust. For example you are putting together your Christmas appeal to send to the printer when a major donor comes in with a friend she is trying to interest in donating to your cause. Drop what you are doing and spend as much time as possible showing this prospect around. More importantly, you want to be sincerely happy the donor brought you this prospect, no matter what it does to your schedule. If you are not happy, you need to reeducate yourself about what your job really is.

John Lennon said, "Life is what happens to us while we're making other plans." An old friend calls to visit when you are involved in a project. Your child wants to show you her new drawing as you are getting dinner ready. These things are not interruptions in our lives but what makes life worth living. Many of the great chances to give real charity come on the spur of the moment. We have to understand that the eternal only breaks into our present, never our plans for the future. The encounter with God will only happen in the here and now.

Focus on the Donor: Let the other people in your organization worry about the cause, the needy client, the goal. You need to stay focused on the donor and the donor's needs. Are you getting feedback from them to help you help them? Are you getting them the information they need to be informed? Are they getting the support they need to be enthusiastic? Are they getting the involvement they need to be committed? In other words, are you maintaining the relationship? You had better be, because they are the lifeblood of the charity.

A professional beggar can put up a pretense of being a caring person but in the long run it will be easier to develop a warm and caring personality than live a life of professional hypocrisy. In your personal life, are you the sort of person who is interested in others or only interested in what others can do for you? Do you think you are the most fascinating person you have ever met and are you annoyed at others failure to agree with this? Do you think the world owes you money, happiness or recognition?

If you said "yes" to any of those questions you might want to do an experiment. Try living for three months as if all those statements were answered "no". Seek out interesting aspects of other people. (The best way is to listen to them talk.) Find someone to admire and view as a hero. Look for opportunities to learn from others. Rest assured, no one would ever criticize you for taking a sincere and loving interest in him or her. At the end of the three months, try it for another three months. Continue this process until the wonder and delight of it fills your life.

Remember, a great beggar is one who will always say "thank you" to the donors. Say, "thank you", say "thank you", say "thank you", say "thank you", say "thank you"!!! You cannot say it too often. You cannot say it too loudly. Remember that the donors do not owe you the money and a "thanks" is all they are getting. Don't ever forget. It is the most important rule of all. So tell the donors, "thank you".

In life there is much we are not grateful for. Pain is real. Sorrow is real. Loss is real. Death is real. I would never be so coldly shallow and insensitive as to tell someone in the midst of their suffering to be happy and grateful. Jesus wept over Lazarus. He did not put on one of those yellow "smiley face" masks. However, for most of us there is a time of joy as well as a time of sorrow. Birds sing, even on battlefields, and flowers will bloom on graves. So, when you can experience joy, try offering thanks. You can say "thank you", you can sing "thank you", you can laugh "thank you", you can dance "thank you", you can even dream "thank you". It can flow out of you like living water.

Fellow beggars, remember the traditional response to "thank you" is "you are welcome". Every change of the seasons, every star in the sky, and every atom in the cosmos exists to respond "you are welcome". You are welcome in the now and in the eternal.

Acknowledgments

I am very grateful to the friends and family members who helped make this book a reality. My old friend Steve Elmore repeatedly edited this work and both he and Linda Wiener contributed their viewpoints and insights to help me flesh out many of my ideas. Steve also kept pushing me to improve what I was writing. I am fortunate to have such friends.

Nicole and Douglas Lewis did the first edit and gave me an honest evaluation of what I was attempting. Nichole designed the cover and Douglas led me through the confusing path of getting the manuscript into a form Amazon could use. Both of them were very busy at the time and I am delighted they were so cheerful about helping.

In addition, I want to offer my thanks to all the great professionals in the St. Louis charitable world. I have learned so much from the members of the Association of Fundraising Professionals, the St. Louis Planned Giving Council and the Community Service Public Relations Council. This book is my small way of thanking them for all the help they gave me over the years.

Finally, I want to acknowledge the volunteers, donors, board members and especially the staff of Kingdom House. Kingdom House has played a positive role in the St. Louis community for over 100 years. It was an honor and a privilege to work with them. They are some of the finest people I know.

www.ingramcontent.com/pod-product-compliance
Lightning Source LLC
Chambersburg PA
CBHW072258210326
41519CB00057B/1763